Residential
LIGHTING DESIGN

MARCUS STEFFEN

Residential
LIGHTING DESIGN

MARCUS STEFFEN

THE CROWOOD PRESS

First published in 2014 by
The Crowood Press Ltd
Ramsbury, Marlborough
Wiltshire SN8 2HR

www.crowood.com

British Library Cataloguing-in-Publication Data
A catalogue record for this book is available from the British Library.

ISBN 978 1 84797 756 4

Dedication
This book is for my wife and children, whose love and support bring me inspiration
every day.

Acknowledgements
I would like to thank John and Leigh Everett of Mr Resistor. Without them starting me on
the path to being a lighting designer I would never have had this chance to write a book.
They shared their vast knowledge and gave me freedom to create and make mistakes,
learning in the process. I have been allowed to learn and progress with their support and
help. Thank you for my wonderful clients, who let me into their lives and homes, and
allowed me such a personal view into how they live. Without willing clients who also have
a passion for lighting I would not be able to create good lighting designs. Thank you to
Alan Hughes and Atousa who gave me the opportunity to lecture at the Inchbald School
of Design. They have been helpful and supportive and given me the wonderful task of
introducing interior designers into the world of lighting. Finally, thank you to my wife,
Emanuela, for her patience and understanding in the time I needed to write this book. She
has supported me and helped take care of our family while I have sat trying to convey my
thoughts onto paper.

Disclaimer
This book is intended for guidance on wiring and installation only. Regulations do change
over time, and all lighting should be installed by qualified professionals to the latest set of
standards. Wiring diagrams are presented to give knowledge of the principle of installation,
and all installations should refer to the manufacturer's specified installation diagrams. The
author and publishers accept no responsibility for incorrect installation or wiring.

Typeset by Jean Cussons Typesetting, Diss, Norfolk

Printed and bound in Singapore by Craft Print International

CONTENTS

1   The Nature of Light   7

2   Lamps   13

3   Light Fittings   27

4   Basics of Lighting Design   47

5   The Heart of the Home: the Kitchen   69

6   Luxury and Style: the Bathroom   85

7   Comfort and Relaxation: the Living Room   103

8   Entertaining with Drama: the Dining Room   117

9   The Retreat from the World: the Bedroom   127

10 Lighting Controls   139

11 Creating a Lighting Plan   153

Index   159

CHAPTER 1

THE NATURE OF LIGHT

Light is a complex medium with which to work. While light itself is understood by science, how it is perceived by humans is still not fully comprehended. Different people react to light in different ways, and it is important to be sensitive to what people like and dislike with certain properties of light.

OPPOSITE: LED strip set into a recess under the handrail illuminates the stairs, while pendants and wall lights provide general and effect lighting within the space.

BELOW: LED lighting in a living room with an LED strip used as a guide light inthe hallway. (Photo: Mr Resistor)

Light, and this book deals only with visual light, is the emission of energy within a certain bandwidth range, known as the visual spectrum. The range of wavelengths is generally between 390nm and 700nm, though this can vary depending on the person. Light can be received directly from a light emitter, such as a lamp, but it can also be seen as a reflection from other objects. The colour of objects is determined by the light that is reflected from their surfaces, and thus received by the eye.

Light travels in straight lines, and so it is easy to predict where light will fall within a room. Standard mathematics can

be used to determine if a light source will be visible and have a high glare, or if light will fall on a particular surface. When light travels through different materials, such as air and glass, then the direction of the light will change. Most of the time this is not relevant, but when lighting glass it is important to remember the principle of total internal reflection. If the light contacts the glass at a very shallow angle, almost parallel with the surface of the glass, then it will not penetrate it, but reflect off it and away, similar to a mirror. This is important to note, since in some cases it will not be possible to light through a piece of glass, such as a step, if the light is being transmitted next to it.

PROPERTIES OF LIGHT AND ELECTRICITY

Luminous Intensity

Luminous intensity is the measure of visible light in a particular direction per solid angle. The SI unit for luminous intensity is the candela (cd). This gives a good indication of the intensity of the light emitted from a lamp. Most lamps with a beam angle (generally up to 60°) will have a peak intensity, or candela, value. This allows comparison between different lamps with a beam angle and gives an idea of the maximum light output.

Luminous Flux

Luminous flux is the measure of the visible light output of a light source (a lamp). The SI unit for luminous flux is the lumen (lm). Whereas luminous intensity deals with visible light emitted in a particular angle, luminous flux is the light emitted all around a light source. The lumen value is generally given for unidirectional lamps, such as fluorescent tubes and standard incandescent lamps. This is another way of comparing the light output between different lamps to see which is brighter.

OPPOSITE: Daylight being broken as it passes through crystal door handles. (Photo: Marcus Steffen)

Illuminance

Illuminance is the measure of luminous flux per unit area. The SI unit for illuminance is lux (lx). One lux is equal to one lumen per square metre. In most homes an illuminance level of between 100lx and 500lx is required, depending on the different areas in the home. A house would not be lit with 500lx through its entirety, as this may only need to be achieved on some work surfaces. Most residential lighting designs do not need or want measured illuminance levels, but it may be helpful to compare different lamps and the actual light output. Most lamp manufacturers produce a light cone, which shows the peak illuminance at different distances. These provide a quick comparison of the actual light output from a lamp, and show which is brighter.

Power

Power in lighting refers to the electrical power used by the lamps in the system. The SI unit of power is the watt (W). Almost all equipment will have a maximum wattage that it can control. Some will have a minimum wattage as well. It is important that these limits are observed, since if they are exceeded then it could mean early failure of either the light fittings or the equipment. For example, many dimmer switches have a maximum wattage of 250W. If the lighting circuit carries more than 250W, for example three 100W incandescent lamps, then this could cause the dimmer to overheat. It is normally acceptable to have less than the maximum wattage on lighting equipment, unless it is a fluorescent or metal halide lamp, in which case it must be matched.

Efficacy

Efficacy is similar to efficiency, but is the ratio between two figures with different units. In lighting terms, efficacy relates to the lumen to watt ratio. This is a common way of measuring how low energy a light source is. It is the number of lumens emitted divided by the number of watts of power consumed, and is noted with the unit lm/W. There are different variations of the lm/W ratio. Some take into account the power losses of transformers and ballasts used by a light fitting (commonly noted as a circuit watt), and some also take into account the light lost when a lamp is fitted into a light fitting (the luminaire lumen value as opposed to the lamp lumen value).

Electric Potential

Electric potential is measured in Volts (V). An electrical circuit will have a voltage associated with it. In most cases this matches the national voltage, provided by electric companies to homes. In the United Kingdom this is 230V AC, whereas the United States uses 120V AC. There are variations across the world, so if light fittings are being purchased from other countries, it is important to ensure that they will work in the installation.

Current

Current is the flow of electric charge. The SI unit of current is the amp (A). There is a maximum amount of current that can be taken into a home, and this in turn limits what can be used for lighting. There is a maximum amount of power that a dimmer switch can handle, which is related directly to the maximum amount of current that can flow through that dimmer switch. Current, Voltage and Power are all inherently related to one another, and if two values are known then the third can be calculated using the formula Power = Voltage x Current. In some cases, such as with on/off switches, there will not be a maximum wattage but rather a maximum current, commonly 10A. It is worth being aware of the different values required and how to find them out.

LEDs generally require a constant current to make them emit the maximum possible light. Rather than a specified voltage, like most other lamps have, many LEDs have a specified current, such as 350mA or 700mA. It is important to obtain an LED driver that matches this to enable them to work at maximum efficiency, and avoid damaging the LEDs.

Correlated Colour Temperature

The correlated colour temperature (CCT) of a lamp is the measure of the warmth of the light emitted from it. It is measured in Kelvin (K). Incandescent lamps have a colour temperature of 2700K, whereas fluorescents can have colour temperatures ranging from 2200K (orange/white) to 8000K (blue/white).

Ensuring that the correct colour temperature is used is essential to any lighting design. If cool colours are used in rooms for relaxation then they will look harsh and uninviting. If warm colours are used exclusively then the rooms

The range of colour temperatures of white. (Photo: Marcus Steffen)

COLOUR TEMPERATURES
2200K – Orange/White
2700K – Interna (incandescent and mains voltage halogens)
3000K – Warm White (low-voltage halogen)
3500K – Neutral White
4000K – Cool White (commonly used in offices and shops)
6500K – Daylight (used in offices, very cold with blue tones, closest to daylight)
8000K – Blue/White (very cold white, with a lot of blue in the colour)

may appear dirty and old. Finding a balance between different colour temperatures can be quite difficult and it is worth experimenting with different lamps of different colours to find the right combination.

As a general rule, if a high level of light is required, it should be cooler. Utility rooms, for example, work very well with a very bright light at the 3500K–4000K CCT range. If a lower level of light is required, say for a bedroom, then warmer colour temperatures should be used, between 2700K and 3200K. It is acceptable to have different colour temperatures within one room, and they can work well together, but if two light sources are serving the same purpose, such as illuminating a work surface, then their colour temperature should be matched. However, if the surfaces being lit are different colours, then it may be acceptable or desirable to have two different colour temperatures lighting them. Just as with paint and fabrics within a room, the colour temperature is something that needs to be tailored to the room and matched to the décor.

It is important to note that lamps with a filament change colour as they are dimmed. As the filament cools, it will go from emitting a cooler white light to emitting colours more in the yellow and amber ranges. Incandescents and halogens all become warmer as they dim. In contrast, LEDs maintain the same colour temperature no matter what the brightness.

This is important to bear in mind when choosing the lighting within a room, since an LED may not be able to provide both a clean, bright light in the cooler ranges and a warmer tone when dimmed. It may be necessary to use other light sources to achieve this warmth, such as table lamps with shades and incandescent lamps. Fluorescents are even more unpredictable, with some fluorescent lamps emitting a cooler colour temperature when dimmed.

Colour Rendering Index

The colour rendering index (CRI) is a measure of how well a light source matches a particular spectrum standard called a black body radiator. An incandescent lamp will match the black body radiator, and has a CRI of 100. It is used as a guide to how well light shows colours on a surface. A good example of a very low CRI lamp are the sodium lamps used in some street lighting, giving an orange/yellow light. It is almost impossible to discern different colours below one of these lamps, since they all look the same, and these have a negative value CRI. The CRI of a lamp is a good measure of how well the lamp will show colours. If the CRI rating is in the 90s, then this is exceptionally good; if it is in the 80s it will be good, but not amazing. Anything below 80 is not really suitable for residential use.

CHAPTER 2

LAMPS

There are numerous different types of lamp on the market, each with its own benefits and problems. From the humble incandescent lamp to the LED, the range is wide and bewildering. Most people refer to them as bulbs, but within the lighting industry the correct term is lamp. This can lead to some confusion between lighting specialists and their clients. Choosing the correct lamp forms an essential part of creating a good lighting design for the home. If the wrong colour or beam width is used, it can ruin the atmosphere of a room, and can even make a space unusable. The correct lamp will enable everything to work as intended, and enable a house to become a home.

This section discusses the different types of lamp, and lists the different characteristics that need to be taken into account. This will act as a guide to what information to look for when choosing lighting for the home, and ensuring that the product is supplied as intended.

INCANDESCENT

The incandescent lamp has been available for over a hundred years. Designed with a tungsten filament heated up to burn brightly, it has formed the basis of electrical lighting since it became available. Its warm glow has brought about revolutions in lifestyle and it has become a design icon in its own right. It is both loved and hated for a number of reasons, and has latterly come to be regarded as a symbol of inefficiency as global warming has become a central issue in the world.

ABOVE: A decorative incandescent lamp with an extended filament. (Photo: Mr Resistor)

OPPOSITE: A small LED spotlight illuminates a crystal decanter, with beautiful patterns created from the refraction of the light through the crystal.

A selection of different incandescent lamps with different lamp holders. (Photo: Mr Resistor)

Incandescent lamps produce light by heating a wire to a high temperature, causing it to glow white hot. The repeated heating of the filament means that the lamp normally has a short life, of between 500 and 1500 hours. Longer-life versions have been made, but generally manufacturing methods and cost have meant that they became niche products. In addition, incandescent lamps do not have a good efficacy rating. A lot of the energy provided by the electricity goes into heat generation, while only a small portion is given out as light in the visible spectrum. These lamps give out a broad, mostly even spread of light in the visible spectrum, with slightly more red and yellow light emitted, giving them their distinctive warm colour (2700K). Due to its wide spectrum of light emission, the incandescent lamp is also closest to the ideal light source for the Colour Rendering Index, giving it a CRI rating of 100. While CRI is not a perfect way of measuring how colour appears on objects, it does give a guideline. Comparisons between colour temperature and CRI can help determine how close other sources of light are to incandescent light.

The incandescent lamp has been the main source of light for almost all homes over the last century, and has become integrated into the psyche of humans. The warm light it gives has carried on the image of fire in creating a warm atmosphere to return to after a hard day's work. Creating a safe, inviting haven away from the world is the aim of the home, and this warm light forms part of that image. While rising energy costs mean this lamp is becoming much more scarce, it is essential to know the type of light that is generated from it since it has formed the basis of residential lighting for the last hundred years.

TUNGSTEN HALOGEN

Tungsten halogen lamps are normally used in directional reflector types, commonly known as low-voltage halogen or halogen spotlights. Using an extra halogen component inside the lamp's make-up enables it to burn at much higher temperatures, producing more light, and it lasts longer than normal

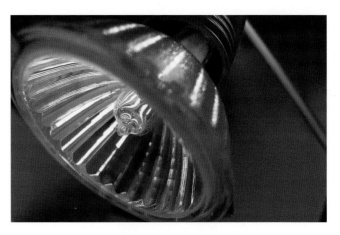

A close-up of a halogen dichroic lamp, showing the centre capsule lamp and the reflector. (Photo: Mr Resistor)

incandescent lamps. The majority of these lamps come with a reflector, focusing all the emitted light into a beam. This enables light to be concentrated on a point rather than diffused in all directions. They are normally available in a large range of different beam angles, from as narrow as 8° to as wide as 60°. Due to the higher temperature at which the filament burns, most halogen lamps will not work on normal household voltage. They require a transformer to reduce the voltage down to between 12V and 24V, depending on the lamp type. This increases the current through the lamp, and this enables the filament to reach maximum temperature.

GLS			E27 (ES)
ROUND			E14 (SES)
CANDLE			E12 (CES)
PYGMY			E10 (MES)
TUBULAR			B22 (BC)
CROWN SILVER			B15 (SBC)

Common incandescent lamps and lamp holders. (Diagram: Marcus Steffen)

The colour of halogens is similar to that of incandescent lamps. Low-voltage halogens are normally slightly cooler, producing light with a colour temperature of around 3000K. As with incandescent lamps, the light colour changes if they are dimmed, with the colour temperature varying from 3000K down to 2000K–1500K at the lowest levels.

Halogen lamps with reflectors form a major part of a lighting designer's toolbox. The control that this gives over light

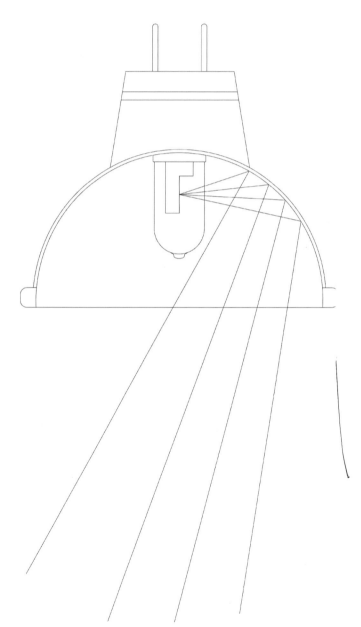

Diagram showing how a dichroic reflector focuses and controls the light into a beam. (Diagram: Marcus Steffen)

and where it is applied to the surfaces of a room can enable the tailoring of light to a particular situation and gives a large amount of flexibility in how light is used. They enable good task lighting onto work surfaces, or can be used to highlight artwork or sculpture. They can also be used to provide general light throughout a space.

Most halogen lamps come with a 50mm dichroic reflector with the MR16 shape. There are also smaller versions (35mm and 25mm diameter), with MR11 and MR8 bodies respectively. All of these use a dichroic reflector, made of glass. This is used to reflect the light forward into a beam, while allowing the heat to escape out of the rear of the lamp. This prevents the heat being projected forward, causing heat gain in a room and making it uncomfortable to remain underneath the spotlights for a long period of time. There are specialist versions of this type of lamp, known as Reflekto or heat forward lamps, which have coatings that project the heat out of the front of the lamp. These are normally used in specialist fittings that either are enclosed at the rear, or have delicate electrics behind the lamp mounting position. Care should be taken when replacing these lamps to ensure the correct type – heat forward or backward – is supplied, since damage could be done to the light fittings if the incorrect type is installed.

Less common types of halogen lamp are the AR111 and AR70 ranges. These are commonly known as anti-glare bar lamps. Sometimes the notation of QR111 or QR70 is used, but they refer to the same lamp. Instead of a glass reflector these use a metal reflector. In addition to this, the halogen capsule lamp that provides the light is covered by a cap (held by a bar, hence the name 'anti-glare bar lamp'). This means that the halogen capsule is not visible, and this reduces the glare from the lamp. The light is reflected from the metal reflector out into the room. This has the effect of giving a soft light. The nature of the metal reflector means that it allows tight control over the beam angle, with narrow beam lamps achieving a 4° beam angle. These lamps are typically found in museums and art galleries due to the precise control they can achieve, allowing the light to be directed onto specific items or artworks. They are also fantastic for both general light and spotlighting of artwork in the home, especially where there are high ceilings, since they are available in higher brightness versions than the normal dichroic lamps.

Newer halogen lamps sometimes come in a special version, known as IRC (Infra-Red Coating). These lamps are more efficient due to a special coating over the internal surface of the halogen capsule lamp, which reflects the infra-red light range

The Art Cabin in Southfields, London, using AR111 lamps to focus light onto artwork. (Photo: Mr Resistor)

back into the capsule lamp, allowing it to burn at higher temperatures and producing more light. With the modern requirements for higher efficiency lamps, these are becoming the standard lamp.

The majority of halogens used are the reflector types discussed above, but there is another range of halogen capsule lamps that are used either in very small fittings, such as those positioned under kitchen cupboards, or in specialist track-mounted lights for illuminating artwork. The fittings for these lamps are normally supplied with custom-made reflectors to aim the light in a particular direction, and give very good beam control. The most common base types are the G4, the GY6.3 and the G9. The G4 and the GY6.3 are both low-voltage versions, requiring a transformer to operate. The G9 is a mains voltage lamp, meaning no transformer is required

to use it. This type of lamp is also becoming popular for use in wall lights, after the banning of standard non-directional incandescent lamps.

LIGHT EMITTING DIODES

Light Emitting Diodes (LEDs) have been around for over fifty years. They were originally used as indicator lights on almost all electrical equipment, but since the discovery of the blue LED, followed by a coating technique to obtain white light, they have been seen as the future of lighting. Extremely efficient, and with a wide range of colours, this is the fastest-growing area of lamp development in the lighting industry.

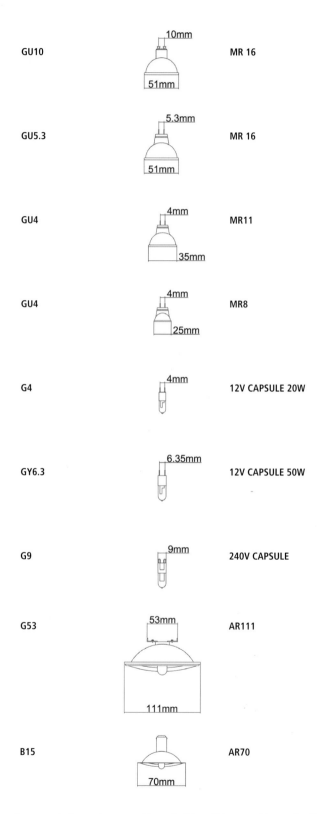

GU10		MR 16
GU5.3		MR 16
GU4		MR11
GU4		MR8
G4		12V CAPSULE 20W
GY6.3		12V CAPSULE 50W
G9		240V CAPSULE
G53		AR111
B15		AR70

Common halogen lamps and lamp holders. (Diagram: Marcus Steffen)

The potential for both reduced energy consumption and reduced waste means that LEDs will be the future of lighting in the world. There is a wide variety of LEDs available on the market, and care must be taken when selecting which one to use in a project. The fact that they are being constantly developed, and more efficient versions released, means that there is no set 'standard' on the market, and so each one must be analysed to see if it gives the desired light.

LEDs are fixed to a circuit-board of some description, and normally other electrical components are required. In general, a single LED will have a beam angle of between 110° and 140°. Almost all LEDs are sold in a body of some description, be it on a long strip with multiple LEDs, or in a lamp form with reflectors to focus the light. They almost always require a transformer of some type, depending on the kind of LED being used. When referring to LEDs, the transformer is normally known as an LED driver so as to avoid confusion with low-voltage halogen transformers. Sometimes LED lamps will work on mains voltage, but this normally means that the driver is built into the body of the lamp.

LEDs come in a wide variety of colours, including many whites. The first White LEDs were a very cold, white light, with a colour temperature of around 6500K–8000K. This is almost a blue/white colour, due to their development from Blue LEDs. With the development of the technology, there are now LEDs available in whites from very warm (2700K) to very cold (6500K) and many in between. Unfortunately the manufacturing process of LEDs means that accurate colour matching between batches is very difficult to achieve. There are always variations between batches, and even within batches. Manufacturers use a binning method, selling LEDs in colour bins of colour temperatures. Purchase of LEDs can be made from a very narrow bin range, resulting in high cost, but good colour temperature matching, or from a wide range of bins, meaning that there will be a reduced cost, but wider-ranging colour temperatures on the LEDs purchased.

LEDs are also available in colours, the most common of which are red, green, blue and yellow/amber. Sometimes single-colour LEDs are used to provide an accent light or they are used as marker lights. Red, green and blue LEDs are also combined into light fittings which allow the mixing of these three colours. These are known as colour-changing or RGB lights. Since almost any colour can be produced by mixing red, green and blue, they can be used to create colour-changing fittings to add fun or dramatic lighting to an installation. However, while the RGB lights can produce a huge

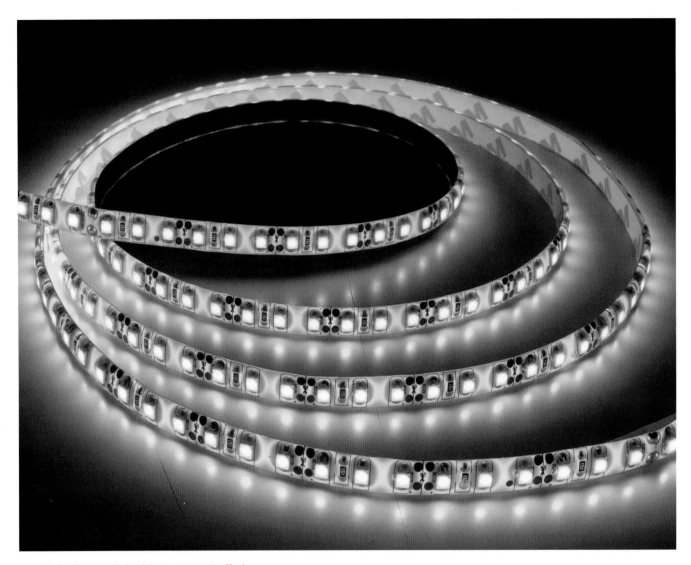

An LED flexible strip light. (Photo: Marcus Steffen)

range of colours, they are not particularly good at producing whites. White requires a very broad spectrum of light, and the narrow-spectrum bands of the red, green and blue make it difficult to produce a wide enough spectrum. Some RGB lights incorporate a cool white or warm white LED so that white light can also be obtained from the same fitting. Care should be taken when using coloured LEDs to ensure that they do not clash with the interior design in which they are placed, though they can be a great asset when used correctly.

LED lamps have the potential to be dimmed. LEDs them-

selves rely on a certain amount of current from the LED driver to work at maximum brightness, and reducing this current reduces the amount of light emitted. The key to dimming LEDs is to have an LED driver that can be dimmed. As well as the standard phase dimmers found in most houses, there are more specialist dimmers available that might be required, depending on the LED driver being used. The common dimmer types used for LEDs are 0–10V, DSI, DALI and DMX. It is important to note that all these alternative dimming types require extra wiring to be installed in a property, different from standard cables installed by electricians. It is essential

T5 fluorescent lamps.
(Photo: Mr Resistor)

to make sure that the type of dimming is known before the wiring is done in a property so that the correct cables are installed for the LED types being used.

Unlike incandescent and halogen lamps, LEDs do not become warmer when they are dimmed. They remain at their set colour temperature, simply reducing the light output. The majority of people are used to this change in colour, achieving that warmer, 'cosier' atmosphere in a room, so using LEDs will give a different light that some may not like. Some LED light fittings incorporate a variety of white LEDs, and vary the brightness of each of them as they dim, simulating the effect of incandescent lamps.

LEDs generally have a very long lifetime, between 20,000 and 50,000 hours. The key to a long lifetime is correct cooling for the LEDs. While LEDs do not give off heat like an incandescent or halogen lamp, they do produce high heat on the circuit board on which they are mounted. High temperatures reduce the life of the LED, so correct heat removal is very important. The long life of LEDs means that there can be large cost savings in using them, in terms of both energy consumption, and in reduced maintenance and replacement costs.

There are two types of LED lamp available on the market. The first are high-output individual LEDs, which are normally used as spotlights or floodlights. These run at a very high constant current, and output a large amount of light for one LED.

They are used in retro-fit LED lamps for downlights, as well as dedicated downlights with the LEDs built into the body of the fitting. They require heat sinks to remove the heat generated by the electrical current on the PCB. These can vary wildly in size, and all depend on the design and circuit construction of the LED itself. A good heat sink is very important, since it cools the LED itself, which will extend the life of the lamp. A poorly cooled LED will have a much shorter life, which could drastically reduce any predicted savings over the long-term life of a project.

The second type of LED is a small, standard output one, used in large groups to produce light. These are commonly used for creating long strips of LEDs. While each LED is less powerful than a high-output LED, many more can be fitted onto a circuit board, which can even be made to be flexible. LED strips are used for linear lighting solutions, such as under cupboards and plinths, and in furniture. They have a wide spread of light which enables them to wash surfaces with light.

FLUORESCENT

Fluorescent lamps are commonly found in commercial properties, but their use in residential lighting has increased greatly due to high energy costs. Their technology has improved a vast amount since the days of flickering tubes casting a cold, uninviting light around a room. Now fluorescents are available in a range of colours, and with the development of modern ballasts (the fluorescent equivalent of a transformer) the flicker is all but eliminated.

Fluorescent lamps work by passing an electrical current through a gas, reversing the direction of travel of the current thousands of times a second. Light is generated through the reaction of the gas, and a coating on the glass tube. The light emitted from tubes is given out in all directions evenly, creating a general distribution of light that is difficult to achieve with incandescent or LED. Fluorescent lamps also have a high light output for a low power input, giving it a high efficacy.

Fluorescents are available in a wide range of colour temperatures, from 2200K (extremely warm, almost orange) to 6500K (ice-cold blue/white, associated with daylight). This gives a wide choice of colours to match interior decoration and style. Most of the time warmer colours are used (2700–3000K), but sometimes 4000–5000K colours can be good in very dark, cold-coloured interiors.

Fluorescents can be dimmed, but require a special ballast and extra wiring. The most common way of dimming in residential properties is 0–10V, though sometimes other methods are used. No matter which method is used, it is important that this aspect be considered early on in a project, since it cannot be changed at a later time without resulting in significant work. It should be noted that the colour can vary slightly with fluorescents when dimming. They sometimes become slightly cooler or warmer, depending on the colour type and the composition of the tube. Fluorescents cannot normally be dimmed lower than 10 per cent, since the tube will begin to flicker. If very low levels of light are needed then it would be best to consider an LED light source instead.

There are number of different fluorescent lamps available. The most common type is a retro-fit lamp for screw or bayonet lampholder. These give a good light, but are generally not dimmable. The fluorescent ballast is placed in the body of the lamp, hence they are larger than incandescent lamps. They come in a range of different colour temperatures, but 2700K is by far the most common. Standard edison screw (E27) and bayonet (B22) versions are available, but smaller versions are also made: generally the small edison screw (E14) and small

T5 – 16mm diameter

T5 Lamps		
Length	High Efficiency Wattage	Wattage
300mm	8W	–
563mm	14W	24W
863mm	21W	39W
1163mm	28W	54W
1449mm	35W	80W

T8 – 25.4mm diameter

T8 Lamps	
Length	Wattage
600mm	18W
900mm	30W
1200mm	36W
1500mm	58W
1800mm	70W

Chart showing the different lengths, wattages and lamp holders of standard linear fluorescents. (Diagram: Marcus Steffen)

bayonet (B15). It is important to check the size of the whole lamp when looking at the smaller lamp holders, since a lot of light fittings that use the smaller versions also have little space around them, and the larger body of a retro-fit compact fluorescent lamp will not fit inside.

The retro-fit lamp is a type of compact fluorescent. These are straight fluorescent tubes that are shaped into a more compact size, usually with a number of U bends. As well as the retro-fit types, compact fluorescents also come with dedicated lamp holders. These are used much more in commercial premises, though they have become quite popular as an energy-efficient light in homes, especially when used as wall-mounted uplights. The ballast is located outside the lamp, which allows for a much higher light output and efficiency. It also means that only the matching compact fluorescent lamp can be used. It is not possible to down-rate the lamps, since the ballast is designed to run a particular length and wattage of fluorescent. It is possible to dim a compact fluorescent with a remote ballast, but a resistive or inductive dimmer cannot be used. Generally they are dimmable using SwitchDIM, 0–10V, DSI or DALI. They all require extra cabling and a particular type of dimming control, so it is important that the wiring is allowed for this at the first fix stage of a project to ensure that it is possible. If the wiring has already been done, then a large amount of work will be needed to correct it, since the walls and ceilings will have to be opened up again.

Linear fluorescents can be found all over the world, lighting offices and shops, as well as all manner of other spaces. Linear fluorescents consist of a straight glass tube with end caps and connecting pins at either end. They have a remote ballast that converts the mains power into a usable form for the tube. Linear fluorescents can be mounted on their own, with the ballast positioned some distance away, but it is much more common to find them inside a light fitting, where reflectors and protection can be provided. Linear fluorescents were the first design of fluorescent produced, and as such they are the most developed. They have the best efficacy, and the colour output when trying to achieve warmer ranges is almost com-

A Feelux Slimline tube and fitting, creating a linear light pattern with no dark spots. (Photo: Mr Resistor)

parable with incandescent lamps. Fluorescent lamps are available in a wide variety of lengths and diameters. The two most common diameters are the T8 (25.4mm diameter) and the T5 (15.9mm diameter), and they are available in a range of lengths. The wattage for a tube is related to the length of the tube, for example a 36W T8 fluorescent is 1.2m long, whereas a 58W T8 is 1.5m long. With T5 lamps this can become a little bit more complicated, since there are two ranges, high output (HO) and high efficiency (HE). For every length available there are two different wattages and the correct one must be used. As well as the standard ranges of T5 and T8, there are also a number of manufacturer-specific tubes in the T4 and T2 classifications. There are no standardized lengths and wattages, so when purchasing these specialist fittings, there must be a ready supply of replacement lamps.

Linear fluorescents are used in residential properties, most commonly as concealed uplighters. Multiple lamps are placed in a line to give a linear wash onto a ceiling or wall from either a dropped ceiling detail, or from the top of a bank of cupboards. This produces a soft, indirect wash of light, relying on reflections from the ceiling and walls to light a room. Due to the high light output of the fluorescents, this type of lighting can be used for general light in a room. When designing these features, it becomes even more important to factor the architecture of the building into the layout, since the uplighting highlights this. The lines of linear lighting should follow the lines of the building as much as possible, but sometimes this is not feasible for small turns and recesses owing to the tube length restrictions. It is very important that the lamps cannot be seen from the room, so a pelmet or baffle is normally fitted on the edge of the surface where the fluorescents are mounted. This baffle should be at least as tall as the fluorescent itself, so that it cannot be seen unless a person is above the level of the fluorescent, in which case it is unavoidable. Fluorescent tubes come in fixed lengths, generally varying by 300mm, so achieving a perfect fit for linear uplighting can be quite difficult. Ideally the linear uplighting should be designed around the size of the fluorescent tubes, rather than the other way around, though this is rarely the case. Fluorescents also do not generate light along their full lengths, due to the end caps and lamp holders for electrical connections. This can mean that dark spots may be generated when light fittings are placed end to end. To avoid this problem, fluorescents should be staggered so that an even light is produced. This should be taken into account when calculating the number of fittings needed. It is also important to instruct the contractor to do this work, since it is not always clear, and without proper guidance the tubes may not be installed correctly. There are special 'bent end' fluorescents available on the market, which eliminate this need for staggered fittings. The tube is specially shaped so that the ends turn back on themselves, allowing the lit sections to be positioned right next to each other, thus eliminating dark spots.

COLD CATHODE

Cold cathode lighting, commonly known as neon lighting, is

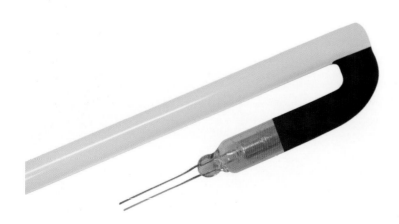

A cold cathode tube, which is normally used in sign making. (Photo: Mr Resistor)

A steam room with a fibre optic star effect ceiling and colour wheel fitted to the light engine. (Photo: Mr Resistor)

sometimes used in residential properties, though it is rare. It uses an inert gas-filled tube with electrodes at either end; electrons are emitted from one end and absorbed at the other. A special coating is used which, when exposed to the electrical current, emits light. These lamps have a very high efficacy and high light output. They can also be made to give almost any white, and a multitude of other colours as well. Each cold cathode tube is custom-made by specialist manufacturers, and can be produced in different diameters, lengths and shapes, from a straight line to a curve or S shape. Generally the manufacturer will come to site to measure up, produce the tubes and install them, since if any part of the process is done incorrectly the tubes will need to be remade, at considerable expense. Due to the custom-made nature of the product it is suitable for unusual installations, such as curves and elaborate shapes, though there is a matching cost to having the cold cathode produced.

Each length of cold cathode requires a neon transformer, which must be placed close to the tube itself, so adequate space needs to be allowed for this within the construction detail. Tubes are available in different diameters, with smaller diameters emitting more light, but they must be run in shorter lengths. Neon transformers can be dimmed, though the required dimming type should be checked with the manufacturer of the transformer, since there is a wide variety on the market. Never assume that they are dimmable.

FIBRE OPTICS

Fibre optics are not strictly a type of lamp, but merely a method of transporting light from one area to another, but they are perhaps best covered as a type of lamp. Fibre optics are solid glass or plastic tubes which are flexible and usually up to 10m long. Different diameters are available, from 0.75mm diameter up to almost any size, though generally they do not go over 5mm of active diameter. Active diameter refers to the actual glass, which emits light. Larger fibres are sheathed in a plastic sleeving both to protect them and to reduce light loss along the length of the fibre. This can be especially important in longer lengths, where light loss can be severe. Fibre optics use the principle of total internal reflection to transmit light from one end. Total internal reflection is a property of light passing through different materials. The light changes path by a certain amount when contacting a barrier between two materials. If the approach angle to the barrier is very small

then the light may be angled at which it turns can cause it to be reflected on the same side of the material it originated from. By projecting light at an almost parallel angle into a fibre optic, the light will continually reflect down its length until it reaches the end, at which point it is emitted, since that end is almost perpendicular to the path of the light. This principle is used with lasers for data communications, but has been subverted to create interesting light fittings.

Fibre optics are most commonly used to create star effects on ceilings, since many of them can be connected back to a single light source. This light source may be either a low-voltage halogen lamp, a metal halide or an LED with a very efficient optic attachment. The small diameter fibres are gathered together in an assembly called a harness, and this is placed into the light engine, which houses the lamp, transformer and normally a variety of coloured lenses. The harness has to be carefully constructed to ensure all the ends of the fibres are positioned correctly to receive the light from the lamp. The ends must all be cut perpendicular to the length of the fibre to allow optimum light transmission. Plastic ones only need to be cut, but glass fibres need their ends polished to ensure good transmission of light. Inside the light engine there is the option to add a colour or twinkle wheel between the lamp and the harness. A colour wheel consists of different-coloured glass segments which, as the wheel rotates, change the colour of the light projected down the fibre optic. A twinkle wheel consists of a metal sheet with slots or holes cut in it. As the twinkle wheel rotates, light is blocked from some of the fibres, giving the effect of the 'stars' twinkling at the other end of the fibre.

Fibre optics can also be used to provide small amounts of task lighting. Plastic is best used for small diameter fibres, where a star effect is wanted, whereas glass fibres are much better at transmitting light and are available in much larger diameters. These can generally be found in jewellery cabinets and display cases, especially where heat is a problem. The light engine can be located in the plinth of the cabinet, and the light transmitted via the fibre up to the display area. This allows for lots of very small spotlights, allowing for the display of more products. In a residential property they can be used to provide light to awkward or hard-to-reach areas, or positions with high moisture levels. Since the fibre is not a lamp itself, it does not need changing, but rather the lamp in the light engine does. This makes it an excellent light source for lighting little alcoves and details that would be difficult to reach for maintenance. They are also a good light source for use in steam rooms, where, since the moisture levels are so high, most light fittings do not have the correct protection.

METAL HALIDES

Metal halides are discharge lamps that can produce large amounts of light with a very high efficacy. The colour rendering index of metal halides is very good, and their first purpose when produced was to provide light for colour matching for fabrics in textile factories. They are commonly used in shops and galleries but they are not suitable for home use. Due to the way in which light is generated in metal halides, they require a two- to three-minute start-up time. During this period the colour of the lamps varies wildly and there will be flickering. When metal halides are switched off, the lamps need to cool down before they are restarted, which can take up to ten minutes. For these reasons metal halides are not suitable for use in residential properties. Occasionally they can be used for external lighting, especially for large trees or garden structures, since they will not need to be switched on and off very often. They are included here for the sake of completeness.

CHAPTER 3

LIGHT FITTINGS

Light fittings are not themselves light sources, but are both the fixing for the lamp and the tool that gives the lamp its purpose. The lamp and light fitting are intrinsically linked and both must be correct to give the right light into a space. Poorly designed light fittings prevent a lamp from giving the correct light, while a light fitting with the incorrect type of lamp is just as ineffective. The light fitting controls and shapes the illumination that is emitted from the lamp. It allows the light to be targeted into specific areas, and can change harsh, glaring lamps into soft, warm, indirect light fittings. It is important that the light fitting and lamp are considered together when creating a lighting design.

PENDANTS

Pendants are a staple form of lighting that has been around for hundreds of years, pre-dating electricity and even gas. The idea of a central light fitting within the room is as old as fire itself, and can be found in almost every home. With the invention of the incandescent light bulb it became common to place a single hanging lamp in the centre of a room. This was not for decorative purposes, but due to the high cost of electricity. Some old pendant fittings carried plugs to power appliances, since plug sockets were an extra cost. Unfortunately the pendant in the centre of a room is not a good way of lighting the space, but it has become so ingrained in construction that it is thought of as acceptable. A central pendant casts shadows all around a room, creating dark patches and making the space seem smaller. Nevertheless, while it may not be a good way of lighting a room, a pendant is still an important part of lighting design.

Pendants come in a variety of types, from simple shades to large crystal chandeliers, and from traditional designs to modern, minimalist forms and everything in between. They

OPPOSITE: A dining table lit with multi lamp trimless downlights, while the artwork is highlighted in the background.

LED crystal downlights, creating patterns by refracting the light. (Photo: Mr Resistor)

A feature chandelier suspended over a bath, creating a focal point within the room. (Photo: Mr Resistor)

are as much a part of the interior design within a space as they are a light source. This is a very important factor to consider, and anyone who is involved in the interior design of a property should be involved in the choice of pendants.

Pendants are generally suspended from a base on the ceiling called a ceiling rose. This base allows the cable to be connected inside while concealing the wires. It also provides a support for the pendant to hang from. Some larger pendants require additional support wires as well as the power cable, and heavy pendants may need a reinforced ceiling to support the weight.

Pendants can form a central focal point within a room, but they can also be used in numerous other ways. They provide excellent task lighting when used in rows over a kitchen island or dining table, and they can even be used as bedside lights. When using pendants for task lighting in situations such as these, it is important to ensure that the light spread from

the fitting is adequate. Some pendants only produce a small amount of light, whereas others are specifically designed to focus the light onto a surface. If a pendant is being used for a decorative feature, such as a centrepiece chandelier, it is important to see the light effects that it produces. Shades and glass can change how the light is emitted, so can affect the lighting design for the rest of the room. For crystal this is especially important, since there are many different types and they all give different effects. For example, basic glass differs in how it affects light compared with a Swarovski crystal.

RECESSED DOWNLIGHTS

Downlights are light fittings recessed into the ceiling. The light emitted is directed downwards, and lamps are available

Downlights washing a wall in a repeating pattern, providing a feature to this long, narrow hallway. (Photo: Mr Resistor)

in almost any beam angle, allowing narrow spots and wide floodlights to be created. Downlights are excellent for placing light where it is needed, and can be spread throughout a room lighting desks, kitchen work surfaces, tables or artwork. The different beam angles available in the different lamp types allow the tailoring of light within a room to fit different purposes. For example, a downlight could be used to light a large picture on the wall, and then with a change to a narrow beam lamp, it could also light a sculpture on a table below the picture. Downlights can also be used as a general light source throughout a room. Each downlight will light a certain area and these can be planned out to produce a good light across the room. The number of fittings required will depend on the light output of the lamp used, the beam angle and the height of the ceiling. While lighting software can be used to calculate the lux levels on the floor, this is not normally possible because manufacturers generally do not produce light files for fittings used in residential buildings. Most lamps come with a lighting chart which gives the lux and spread of light at certain heights. This can be used as a guide to how many downlights to have. Note that it is not the downlight that has the details of light output but the lamp itself. As long as the lamp type is fixed, almost any downlight fitting that uses this lamp will give the same light output.

Downlights and Ceiling Construction

Choosing a downlight depends on more than just aesthetic considerations: the construction and installation of the fitting must be checked to see if it is suitable for the area it is to be used in. Downlights are recessed into the ceiling. A hole needs to be cut into the ceiling, and there has to be a cavity behind it to allow for the heat to disperse from the light itself. In the case of a solid ceiling, such as a concrete slab, then it will not be possible to recess the downlight into this sort of surface. Some downlights come with special boxes that can be fitted into a concrete slab when it is poured, but these are very expensive and can be very difficult to incorporate into the structure of a building. It is much easier to fit a suspended ceiling under the concrete one to allow a recess for lighting; this could also conceal pipework and extractor fan tubes.

There are generally two different types of suspended ceiling: metal floating grid ceilings and traditional joisted ceilings. Both of these can be finished with plasterboard, but in older properties a joisted ceiling may have lath and plaster.

Plasterboard is a sheet material which is porous, allowing it to be plastered, producing a smooth finish. Lath and plaster consists of small wooden battens lined up next to each other, which are then plastered. Plasterboard is very easy to cut and fit downlights into, but lath and plaster ceilings are very difficult. When a hole saw is used on them, the laths pull apart and this may crack the existing plaster. Normally a small hole is drilled, and then enlarged by cutting each lath individually. This can be a very time-consuming process and sometimes it is easier to replace the ceiling completely. When positioning downlights, the joist positions should be checked. It is not critical to do this at the design phase, but when it comes to cutting the ceiling it is important that the downlights are not under joists.

Downlights need a certain depth for the body of the fitting and the lamp. This needs to be checked with the ceiling to see if there is enough space for the chosen fitting. Most ceilings have between 100mm and 250mm, though some can be as shallow as 50mm. Halogen fittings need at least 100mm to allow for cooling of the lamps, though 150mm is much better. LED fittings need some space, but some fittings are designed to fit into very small cavity ceilings. Fluorescent downlights generally need a much larger cavity due to the size of the lamps. There should also be a space around the fittings to allow for the cooling of light fittings, and also as an area to locate a transformer or driver. If the ceiling is full of insulation then it must be cleared away around the downlight, or a box should be built above it to keep the insulation away. This can make fitting downlights in ceilings that border external roofs quite difficult, since they need to be well insulated to prevent heat loss.

Most downlights are fitted into the hole in the ceiling with some sort of fixing clip. They are made to be removable in case access is needed, or the fitting breaks and needs to be changed. Certain downlights also require the fitting to be removed from the ceiling to change the lamp. In this case it should be ensured that this is easy to do, since it can become quite a difficult and dirty job if the fixings are not well designed. Some downlights are plastered into the ceiling. This is done to reduce their visibility, since no trims and edges will be visible. This can help hide the downlights so that only the light is visible, and the fittings themselves do not distract from the interior design. Plastered-in fittings must be fitted *before* the ceiling is plastered. Sometimes the ceiling will need to be constructed to hold these fittings, so it is important to know at the design stage if these fittings are to be used.

Fire-Rated Ceilings

Some ceilings require a fire rating to prevent the spread of fire within the building. It is best to check with the architect or builder to find out which ceilings need to be fire-rated. As a general guideline, solid concrete ceilings do not need to be, since they form a fire-rated barrier, but suspended ceilings below a wooden floor above will need to be. In some cases a fire-rated downlight will be asked for. The fire rating does not relate to the downlights, but rather to the ceiling itself. Ceilings are designed to withstand fire penetration for a certain amount of time, normally 30 to 90 minutes depending on the location of the room and the height from the ground. This means that if there is a fire in one room, it will be prevented from spreading through the ceiling above for whatever the rated time is. Unfortunately, when a hole is cut in the ceiling the fire rating is destroyed, so it will need to be reinstated. Fire-rated downlights are fitted with expanding fire retardant materials that will fill the hole when exposed to high temperatures. The downlight's design will be adversely affected with this material though, resulting in a thicker trim around the downlight and restrictions on what lamps can be used inside them. If non-fire-rated downlights are desired, then there are two alternatives to provide a fire rating for the ceiling.

The first alternative to fire-rated fittings is to fit a fire hood inside the ceiling over the hole. This is a flexible cover made of fire-retardant fabric. They are of a specific size to cover a downlight and allow some ventilation around it. Generally they can be fitted through the hole of the downlight, but this can be fiddly to do, and expanding the cover correctly can be quite difficult. Ideally they should be fitted from above, but this is not always possible. It is very important that the fire hood is fully expanded, otherwise it could cause the light fitting to overheat. If there is insulation in the ceiling then this must be cleared away.

The second alternative is to construct fire boxes. The box is made up and fitted over the hole in the ceiling. It must be large enough to allow cooling for the downlight, and provide space for a transformer if one is required. Fire boxes are normally made out of plasterboard, since this is generally the same as the ceiling and is a fire-rated material. This is an ideal solution, but an expensive one. Constructing the boxes can take a long time and cost a lot in labour. Whatever fire-rating solution is chosen, it should be discussed with the installer to ensure that they plan and budget for the method chosen.

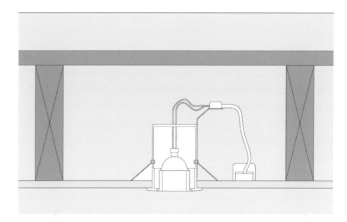

A fire-rated downlight. (Diagram: Marcus Steffen)

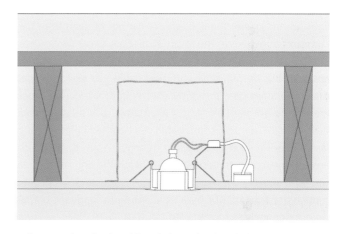

A fire-retardant fire hood fitted above the downlight. Hoods are available in different sizes. (Diagram: Marcus Steffen)

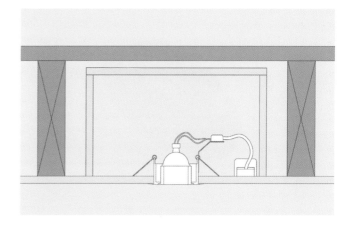

A box constructed of plasterboard forming a fire barrier above the downlight. (Diagram: Marcus Steffen)

Choosing a Downlight

After the ceiling has been checked to ensure that downlights can be fitted, and what sizes are possible, the downlights themselves can be chosen. There are many different types available on the market, ranging from cheap budget fittings to expensive ones adorned with crystals and extra attachments. Finding the right downlight can be quite difficult and some research should be done into different manufacturers and lighting retailers. There are, however, some features to look out for that are common across all manufacturers.

The first important feature is an anti-glare baffle. This little addition helps to reduce the direct glare from the lamp, giving a softer feel to the lighting in a room. It is especially important in rooms with many downlights. An anti-glare baffle normally takes the form of a tube holding the lamp higher within the light fitting, so that the light source cannot be seen from the common sight lines in the room. Baffles are generally finished in black, since this reduces any reflected glare, though fittings are available with chrome and gold baffles, as well as white. Chrome baffles give a slightly cooler light, while gold ones make the light warmer. As an alternative to a fitting with a built-in baffle, a honeycomb baffle can be fitted in front of the lamp. This is a small disc, approximately 3–5mm thick, which has a honeycomb pattern. It helps block the line of sight to the light source, and reduces glare, though such baffles do reduce the light output by a small amount. Standard baffles do not generally reduce the light output.

Another useful feature for a downlight is the ability to adjust the direction in which the lamp faces. This enables the light beam to be moved to different areas and allows the light to be focused where it is needed. If a downlight is fixed in one direction, then the light will only appear there. If the furniture is moved within a room, or the downlight position is altered, perhaps due to a redesign or a problem preventing it being recessed into the ceiling, then the light will fall in the wrong area. For example, a problem might occur if a joist lies in the desired location for a downlight. The downlight will have to be moved, and with a fixed fitting the light will then fall in the wrong place, but with an adjustable one the light can be directed back to the correct target. Normally there is little difference in cost between fixed and adjustable fittings, so it is worth investing a little extra for adjustable ones. There are three common types of adjustable fittings: the eyeball, the gimbal and the scoop.

The eyeball uses a ball and socket joint. The lamp is located within the ball, and can be tilted within the socket of the downlight. This style of downlight has gradually become less common due to the extra size that is required for the fitting.

The gimbal has a ring holding the lamp, and this is hinged along its centre axis. The ring can be tilted in one direction or another, and allows for a maximum of 45° of tilt, though most are limited to 30°. (Any more than this and it would be lighting the interior of the downlight itself.) Some gimbal fittings feature a rotating outer ring to direct the light to left and right, and some have a double gimbal, with the outer ring fitted with its axis perpendicular to the inner ring.

The scoop holds the lamp in a ring which is hinged on one side. The ring can be pulled out of the ceiling, allowing a maximum tilt of 90°, though this can depend on the fitting type. Normally the lamp is enclosed in a body to hide the lamp holder and interior details of the downlight. This fitting is a good option for downlights fitted in a sloped ceiling. The fact that the scoop comes out of the ceiling makes the downlight much more obvious. Scoop fittings are generally larger than gimbal fittings.

An adjustable downlight with a black anti-glare baffle. (Photo: Mr Resistor)

SPOTLIGHTS

Spotlights are light fittings mounted on the surface of a ceiling and they come in an almost endless variety of designs, holding many different types of lamp, so there is normally a spotlight for any situation. Generally they are fitted with

Gimbal downlight. (Photo: Mr Resistor)

A bronze spotlight using a mains voltage halogen lamp. It is able to tilt through 90° and rotate through 360°. (Photo: Mr Resistor)

Eyeball downlight. (Photo: Mr Resistor)

Scoop downlight. (Photo: Mr Resistor)

focused beam lamps, like halogen or LED lamps. They can be used in the same way as downlights to target the light onto particular areas and make them stand out, or there are floodlights that can be used to wash entire areas in a room with an even light.

Spotlights are available in single versions, where one lamp is fitted and can normally be directed in any direction via tilting and rotating. There are also fittings with multiple lamps located on different heads, which are mounted on a base that generally holds them in a line or in a circle. Most fittings have lamps that run on mains voltage, which means there is no requirement for a transformer. As a result, the body of the fitting can be made to almost any shape. If low-voltage lamps are being used, then a transformer of some sort will be built into the body of the light fitting. This results in a larger body to house the transformer.

Spotlights are normally used when it is not possible to recess downlights into the ceiling, either because the ceiling is concrete, or it has a very steep slope. Sometimes spotlights, especially fittings with multiple lamps, are used to replace single pendants as part of some renovation works. This saves having to open up the ceiling to run new cables for downlights. Spotlights are mounted on the surface of the ceiling, so only the power cable will have to be brought through the ceiling.

Choosing a spotlight is a very subjective matter. The whole light fitting is visible, so the design must match the interior design of the room and fit with its style. The colour, shape and finish can all have an effect on how the room is seen, and whether the fittings become an eyesore within the space. Consideration should also be given to the lamps. They are also visible, and should fit with the design of the spotlight. There also needs to be extra protection from glare with spotlight fittings. The lamp can be completely exposed, and spotlights can be angled in any direction, meaning that there is a chance that it could direct light straight into someone's vision. When producing a design, care must be taken to consider where the spotlights will be viewed from within the room and from the entrances. Some spotlights can be fitted with a cowling over the lamp to help conceal the lamp and reduce the glare. Anti-glare lamps, such as halogen bar lamps, are an ideal design for spotlights.

Spotlights can also be fitted with 'barn doors' to help direct the light. These are very common in theatre lighting and consist of four flaps located to the sides of the lamp. They can be folded inwards or outwards, controlling both where the lamp can be seen from and where the light is directed.

TRACK AND WIRE SYSTEMS

Another option for solid ceilings is offered by track and suspended wire systems. These allow some flexibility on where the spotlights can be positioned, and require only one wiring point within the ceiling, making them an excellent choice for retro-fitting into an existing wiring scheme. They also provide a good option for areas where it is difficult to fix spotlights onto a ceiling, such as in glass extensions and high-vaulted

A single circuit track with spotlights used to illuminate artwork. (Photo: Mr Resistor)

ceilings. These systems allow spotlights to be positioned anywhere within a space. Some systems have options for either mounting pendants directly onto them, or powering them while they are suspended from the ceiling separately.

Track Systems

Track systems consist of a long extrusion to which light fittings can be attached. There are specific plugs, known as track adaptors, on each light fitting and this allows them to be fixed anywhere along the length of the track. This gives a vast amount of flexibility in respect of where the lighting can be directed, and enables the lighting layout to be adjusted if the purpose of the room changes. Track lighting is commonly used in art galleries as its flexibility allows the lighting to be adjusted for each exhibition. Using a track system in a residential property can introduce some very interesting possibilities to a lighting scheme. There are many different types of track fitting appropriate to particular styles, giving perhaps a stripped-back industrial feel or lending a futuristic design sense to a room. There are also track fittings that can produce interesting effects, such as gobo and framing projectors.

Many different tracks are available, and they all have different track adaptors for the light fittings. There are two general types of track available: single circuit and three circuit. As their names suggest, the two types refer to the number of circuits that can be controlled on the track. Fittings mounted on a single circuit track will all be switched on and off together. Single circuit track is available in many different designs, and there are both mains voltage and low-voltage versions on the market. Mains voltage track is simple to fit, whereas low-voltage track has smaller fittings, but a transformer must be used to reduce the voltage. Low-voltage track also has a restriction on length, due to the voltage drop inherent in low-voltage circuits. There is also a restriction on the number of fittings, since the transformer's maximum load cannot be exceeded.

Fittings on a three-circuit track can be switched in three distinct circuits, allowing different groupings along the length of the track. Each three-circuit track fitting has a dial on the track adaptor, allowing it to be connected to circuits one, two or three. This track, also known as euro track, is standardized across many manufacturers, giving a much larger range of fittings to choose from. The three different circuits can be used to create different moods from the same light fixtures on the ceiling. For example, circuit one could have spotlights highlighting the artwork in a living room, while circuit two could have spotlights giving a general light, and circuit three could be a feature pendant in the centre of the room. These can all be controlled separately. Three circuit track is a mains voltage, so if low-voltage fittings are being used, they will have an integrated transformer on the body of the fitting. A three-circuit track requires extra cables to be connected to it, since it is effectively three distinct circuits. The electrician must be made aware of this before the first fix is done so the correct cable can be allowed for.

FRAMING AND GOBO PROJECTORS

Framing and Gobo projectors are specialist spotlights used for controlling and shaping beams of light. A gobo projector uses lenses to focus the light and project it through a silhouette cut-out, called a gobo, projecting this image onto a surface. This could be a logo or picture, but it could also be a pattern, such as leaves or clouds. Multiple gobo projectors can be used to cover a whole wall in a pattern, creating, for example, a forest effect.

Framing projectors use lenses to focus the beam of light, but they use four straight edges to create a rectangle of light on a surface, rather than projecting through a silhouette cut-out. The edges can be adjusted individually to alter the size and shape of the rectangle. This allows precise lighting of pictures, with only the artwork being lit. Done correctly, it will not look as if the artwork is being lit, but rather the colours will become extremely vivid and stand out much more than before.

Due to the assembly of lenses and attachments, projectors can be quite large, and are normally mounted as spotlights. Some specialist manufacturers make ones that can be recessed in a ceiling, but they are expensive, and require access from above or through a hatch for maintenance.

All track systems are made up of a series of rigid lengths joined together by couplers. Various shaped couplers are available, from standard right angles to T-shapes and flexible types. A grid can be created on the ceiling to ensure that there is coverage of light everywhere within the space. Track can also be cut to a specific length with a saw. The connection point for the track to be wired to (called a live end) is generally located at one end of a length of track, though in some cases the power can be connected into a coupler on the track or have a separate plug-in power cable. Any uncovered ends of a track must be covered with a 'dead end' cap that prevents the exposed electrical rails from being touched, thus avoiding electrocution. Track can be fixed directly to the ceiling, but can also be suspended on wires and rods, allowing it to be floated in high or irregularly shaped spaces.

Wire Systems

Wire systems are similar in many ways to track systems. They can be used to mount different fittings along their lengths, and only need to be wired back to a single connection point, making them a good option for retro-fit installations. Rather than a rigid metal extrusion though, tensioned wires are suspended between two different points, and these carry the electricity. This can allow for a more elegant design in some cases, and also means that only two fixing points are required on opposite sides of a room. Light fittings are fixed to the track by screwing or clipping onto the wires. Unlike the track system, it is not normally possible to move these light fittings once they are fixed in place.

Wire systems are available in both mains and low-voltage

A mono wire suspension lighting system installed in a kitchen where recessing downlights was not possible. (Photo: Mr Resistor)

Simple plaster wall lights that allow light to wash both up and down, creating an indirect light source. (Photo: Mr Resistor)

versions, though the low voltage is by far the most common. A low-voltage system needs a transformer, but the fittings will be much smaller.

As well as two wire suspension systems, there are also single wire systems, where the light fittings are suspended below the wire. Wire systems are secured with tensioners at either end of the length of wire. The wire is cut to the correct length and pulled taut across the space. It is important to have a solid surface for the tensioners to be fixed to so that they do not pull themselves free. This makes wire systems very good for use in rooms with glass ceilings, since they can be suspended across from the walls on either side. If the distance is large, then additional supports may be needed to prevent the wire from sagging. Manufacturers provide guidance on maximum spans before supports are needed. Wire systems can be shaped to

turn round corners. Rigid supports are needed at the corners where the wires turn, and sometimes this will require the wire system to be mounted at a particular height from the ceiling. Careful planning should be done to ensure that the correct fixings and supports are used.

WALL LIGHTS

Wall lights are an excellent option for combining both good lighting and decorative features. Different designs of wall lights can produce almost any desired lighting effect, and there is an endless range of different styles. Unfortunately light emission is rarely considered when purchasing wall lights, and this can be detrimental to a lighting design. At the design stage it is important to consider not just the placement of wall lights, but also the fittings themselves. It is not possible to produce a good lighting design that relies on wall lights for illumination without knowing which wall lights will be used.

Wall light positioning can be quite tricky in a lighting design. There may be undetermined positions of furniture, but the wiring locations need to be decided early in the construction process. Sometimes it is necessary to allow wiring at multiple locations, but some of these will be covered up by furniture, and the remaining number will need to provide the necessary illumination. If possible, it is best to confirm furniture positions so that the wall light fittings can be placed in the correct locations.

The height of wall lights can also be quite difficult to determine, and it is important to know the type of light fitting being used before this can be fixed. Most wall lights work at around eye level, but this can be anywhere between 1.4m and 1.9m from the floor with the majority of the population. It is always best to ensure that there is a good distance between the fitting and the ceiling (at least 40cm), and the lights should be placed at a height that is comfortable. If the fitting is closer than 40cm to the ceiling then any light directed upwards will not wash across the ceiling, but rather will create a concentrated pool of light. Even at 40cm some fittings do not work well, so it is best to investigate the spread of light from the fitting before deciding. When measuring the height of fittings it should be done from the finished floor level (FFL), *not* from the foundation level. It is important to specify this to contractors, as otherwise, once the flooring is in place, the wall lights could be 100–200mm lower than originally intended.

Wall lights are normally placed directly in the view of people using a room. They are mounted at eye level, and because of this it is very important to consider the impact glare that these light fittings may have on an environment. Exposed lamps can cause discomfort to someone seated opposite them. Most wall lights are fitted with a shade or cover that reduces or stops the direct glare from the lamp. Some are opaque, resulting in light being emitted in certain directions, while others are translucent to allow some diffusion of light. A decision must be made on how dramatic the contrast of light and shadow is to be within a room. Using a solid shade that only allows light to come from the top and bottom of the fitting will create strong shadows on either side of the light. This may be ideal for an entrance hall, but it is not going to work in a bedroom where a soft, ambient light is desired. The material

from which a shade or cover is made can also affect the light given into a room. A low purity frosted glass shade will colour the light with a green tint, which can be quite unpleasant. A cream fabric shade will introduce a warmer tone to the light, and this can help soften fluorescent and LED lamps. All these elements need to be considered when choosing wall lights.

Wall lights are excellent at creating indirect light to wash off ceilings and provide general light in a room. This has been done for many years with sconce uplights, but now there are different styles of fitting that can be used. If the room is to be lit with wall-mounted uplights, it is important to allow plenty of space between the fitting and the ceiling for the light to spread. The top of the light fitting must also be above the eye line, so generally the top edge must be at least 1.8m from the finished floor level.

LOW-LEVEL WALL LIGHTS

Low-level wall lights are treated differently from other wall lights. These are a newer style of fitting and are used to light floors and stairs by washing light across them. They are similar in principle to wall-mounted uplights, but are inverted and mounted low on the wall. Most fittings are recessed into the wall so that they do not become a trip hazard, though some surface-mounted versions are available. They can be used at intervals on stairs to wash the treads in light, as well as along corridors and landings. They make excellent night lights, since their light output is normally low; if LED fittings are used, they have a very low power consumption.

Fittings normally come in two different varieties. The first has a lamp that shines directly out from the light fitting, perpendicular to the wall in which it is mounted. This emits light the furthest, but can result in a large amount of glare, since the lamp is visible. It is also rather inefficient in terms of its light emission, since half of the light is lost upwards, where it will not have much effect. The second type either angles the lamp itself downwards or has a reflector to direct the light downwards. This type has reduced glare as there is no direct line of sight to the lamp, and better light management, with most of it falling onto the floor surface. The spread of light from this type is not as great, so if there is a large space to be covered, such as a very wide step, then these might not be suitable.

When installing low-level lights that are recessed into the

Small LED spotlights fitted into the stair string, washing steps to provide a guide light. (Photo: Mr Resistor)

wall, the correct fixings *must* be used. Some low-level lights can only be installed in cavity walls, whereas others can be placed in both solid and cavity walls. If the fitting is to be installed into a solid wall, then normally a burial tube or box must be fitted as the wall is constructed, and then the cable can be brought into this space. The fitting then clips into this burial tube or box. Any location below floor level, such as a basement, is always more complicated. Basements have sealed membranes or outer walls, sometimes called tanking, and if this is penetrated it could cause a leak. Low-level lights are sometimes too deep and might penetrate this barrier. If low-level lights are to be used in a basement, it is best to keep them on internal walls so as not to risk damage to the water protection.

When using low-level lights on stairs, it is important to con-sider where they will be seen from, and to take into account the glare from the light fitting. Normally low-level light fit-tings are out of the general eye-line, so glare is not a problem. Fittings on stairs get higher and higher when viewed from the lower floor. If the stairs are enclosed, then this is not normally a problem, but if they are open onto a corridor or room then fittings with reflectors that direct the light downwards and reduce the glare should be used.

As well as individual low-level wall lights, linear lighting can also be used for low-level lighting. Rather than purchasing a light fitting, a recess can be built into the wall to house a light strip, which will give a constant wash of light onto a floor. Linear lights built into the architectural design of the building blend into a space more effectively, thus making them more discreet.

Two table lamps with fabric shades on a console table provide a soft, ambient light and frame a mirror. (Photo: Marcus Steffen)

FLOOR AND TABLE LIGHTS

Floor and table lights are types of light fitting that allow control over what is used. They are powered from plug sockets and can be added even after the project is finished. This allows for lighting effects to be added at the end of the project once the interiors are finished, perhaps to illuminate any features that may have been missed. They can also be used to add extra task lighting or ambient light, or simply as a feature within the room.

When selecting a floor or table light it is important to consider what its purpose will be within the room. If it is to be used for task lighting, then it should be capable of giving a sufficient amount of light onto the target area. If it is being used for ambient light, then it should be dimmable and have the correct colour lamp. Table and floor lights are similar to wall lights in the lighting that they give. They can be fitted with shades of all different materials, and this should be taken into account in the lighting design. Fabric shades can soften and colour the light, while crystal or glass can allow the emission of more light.

Table and floor lights need to be positioned carefully within a room to enable them to be an effective light source. There is no point in allowing for a table light when there will be no table, or putting it in a position where there is no power socket. When creating a lighting design incorporating table and floor lights, it is worth doing the design for the power sockets at the same time. Power sockets should be placed close to the point where the light fitting will be positioned. It is important to make sure that the cable from the socket to the table or floor light does not cross any pathway and thus become a trip hazard. If it is not possible to position the socket on the wall, then it could be placed in the floor. Sockets on the floor should be positioned so that they are covered by furniture such as tables or sofas.

Table and floor lights all work on standard power sockets, but sometimes it is worth using a lighting socket, sometimes called a 5 Amp or 2 Amp socket. These have a different plug from standard power sockets, with round pins, and there will be no switch on the socket plate. All the lighting sockets are wired on a lighting circuit and switched on and off together. This allows the control of multiple table and floor lights, and they can also be dimmed as one circuit. This provides much more control of the light levels from these lights, and is espe-cially useful when a scene- or mood-setting control system is used. The light fittings need to have their plugs changed to match the lighting socket, but this is a simple task that can be carried out by anyone. If lighting sockets are planned, then table and floor lamps with integrated dimmers should not be used. This can cause a clash in the electrical functioning of the dimmer switches, and one or both of them could fail. It may not be possible to dim light fittings that incorporate a touch switch; if these are desired, it should be checked with the manufacturer.

RECESSED UPLIGHTS

Recessed uplights are cut into a floor or shelf, and project light

Recessed uplights set into a staircase, creating a dramatic lighting effect. (Photo: Mr Resistor)

LED strips mounted above door frames providing a soft, indirect light into the hallway. (Lighting design by Chris Millard. Photo: Mr Resistor)

upwards. They are the reverse of downlights, and are generally used for highlighting architectural features and creating interesting effects within a room. They can be used to provide focused beams or wide washes of light onto walls or ceilings. They can also be used for framing doorways, entrances and windows.

Recessed uplights need to be cut into the floor. They have a larger front plate that covers the hole and allows the fitting to rest on top of the floor surface, preventing it from dropping into the cavity below. The floor type needs to be taken into account when choosing whether to use uplights. If a concrete base is being used for the floor, then a cavity will need to be allowed within this. This cavity is normally formed with a burial tube that can be purchased with most uplights. This forms the correct hole for the uplight to be fitted into. Sometimes extra space needs to be provided for transformers or connections, and in this case a larger tube or a box can be fitted. This will be covered by the floor that lies on top of the concrete, though it will not work if the concrete is to be polished as the finished floor surface. If the floor is to be suspended on joists, then uplights can be much easier to fit. A hole can be cut in the top surface, and the uplight will sit within the cavity, along with any connections and transformers.

All recessed uplights must have an IP rating. An IP rating ending in a 4 (IP*4) indicates it will be protected from liquid spills, but for use in bathrooms the IP rating may need to be higher (*see* Chapter 6). If there is a risk of water being spilt around the uplights, then it is best to seal the fitting in with a small amount of silicone. This will prevent water from seeping in around the trim and into the back of the fitting, where it may reach the connections. It needs to be done neatly so that it is not visible.

Recessed uplights are excellent for highlighting features within a room, especially ones on the walls. They can be used to light columns, and door and window frames. This helps highlight these features and draw attention to them. This can be especially effective within a hallway, where there may be many features to light. It is important to have a surface to light onto. If they are used below a window, the light will not show against the glass itself, which is transparent. It will show only on the frame. Thus, for example, it is not worth using uplights to highlight a clear glass balustrade.

Uplights are best positioned close to the feature they are to light. If they are too far away then the light will start too high, and some of the feature will remain unlit. The beam angle of the uplight will show the spread of light it produces, and trigonometry can be used to calculate how far the uplight should be from the feature. Some uplight fittings allow the lamp position to be angled onto a surface, but these are not common. Uplights are completely enclosed to ensure they cannot be penetrated by water, and as a result much more space will be needed within the fitting if the lamp is to be tilted.

If the light fitting is placed close to a surface, then the light will hit it at angles very close to the vertical. This high angle means that the light will create shadows on any areas where there is texture or on surfaces that angle away from the vertical. This can be very effective on raw finishes, such as brick and wood, since the texture will be highlighted and add a lot of visual interest to the wall. Unfortunately this effect will also highlight imperfections in a smooth finish such as plaster. If the plaster is not smooth, then all the raised parts will be highlighted, and the recessed parts will be in shadow. It is important to ensure that the surfaces being lit by uplights are finished adequately so that flaws are not apparent.

LINEAR LIGHTING

Linear lighting, also known as strip lighting, is more of a lighting effect rather than a light fitting. Multiple light fittings are used to create an even wash of light, normally from a concealed location such as the top of a cupboard or under a shelf. The fitting and lamp are not normally visible, so the design and style of the light fitting is not as important as in other cases. Some linear light fittings are little more than a lamp holder and a transformer, so the fitting and the lamp are almost the same thing. In the case of LED strips, the fitting and lamp are almost always combined.

Linear light fittings can be used for a whole range of purposes, and are usually built into the structure of a building or the furniture within it. Built-in lighting is dealt with in more are some important details to consider with all linear lighting.

When concealing linear light fittings it is important to consider where they will be observed from. If they can be seen, then it can destroy the indirect lighting effect. A raised edge is normally fitted in front of the light fittings to prevent them being seen, and this should be at least the height of the fitting to conceal it. If there are highly reflective surfaces around, such as mirrors and gloss floors, then it may be possible to see the light fitting in the reflections. In this case, the light fitting must be hidden with a larger edge on the construction, or fitted with a diffuser to hide it.

Linear light fittings need to provide a uniform output of light along their entire length. It is very important to ensure that there are no breaks in this line of light, and that the same amount of light is produced along its entire length. Some light fittings, such as fluorescents, produce dark spots when put end to end. These occur where the fluorescent tubes end and there is a space for the electrical connections. These dark spots will be very visible on a ceiling, and can ruin the linear lighting effect. When installing linear fittings it is important either to overlap them or to use specialist fittings that are built to eliminate dark spots. As well as the spacing, the light output and colour temperature should be the same for all fittings. If there is any variation, then it may appear as if some of the fittings are failing. If the colour temperature varies along the length, then the location of different light fittings will be quite distinct, and the diffused linear wash will not be uniform.

CHAPTER 4

BASICS OF LIGHTING DESIGN

THE EFFECTS OF LIGHT WITHIN A ROOM

Light is used for different purposes in homes. It is there to provide general light to live by, task lighting to work with and ambient lighting to turn a house into a home. When considering a design for a room, it is beneficial to think about what the purpose of the room is, and what it will be used for. With homes, it is not as simple as just putting a bright light on every surface since this creates a flat and bland feeling. Lighting for the home is about providing atmosphere, and you do this with the play of light and shadow.

Light and Shadow

Getting a good general light is just the start of lighting in a home. Creating texture and depth is far more important, and is what changes a room from bland and boring into a sanctuary from the outside world. The first thing to realize is that you do this by creating different levels of light. While dark shadows are rarely good, soft shadows next to a brightly lit area can help to draw attention to the lit area. The eye is automatically attracted to the brightest, most well lit locations in a room. This factor can be used to make sure that the room's principal features, such as a dining room table or a work of art, are highlighted and become the focal points of the whole space. It also allows unsightly areas to be hidden away by leaving them in shadow. Using light and shadow cre-

ates texture in a room, and having this contrast can act as a decoration all by itself. For example, a simple table lamp with shade controls the light emitted from it, throwing it up and down, while only a small amount comes through the shade to either side. This produces an effect on the wall and can also frame the space between two of them.

Controlled lighting can also be used to expand a space and make it seem larger. Typically a room is lit from the centre by a single pendant, but this creates shadows in all directions as a person moves around the room. It also creates a bright spot in the centre, with the light gradually fading towards the edges. This creates focus in the centre and draws attention away from the walls. To make the room look larger, the walls need to be highlighted with the brightest light. This can be done using wall washing downlights, wall lights that wash light onto the walls or a linear strip along the length of the wall. When entering the room a person's attention is automatically drawn to the surrounding walls, so lighting them ensures that the full size of the room is visible. Light will also be reflected into the room, making sure there is good general light.

Direct and Indirect Light

Two types of light are emitted from a light fitting: direct and indirect light. As their names suggest, direct light shines directly from the lamp into the room, while indirect light reflects off a surface of a fitting or an architectural detail before lighting into the room.

Direct light is brighter since none is lost in reflecting off surfaces. It is normally much more directional, allowing more control of where it goes. Indirect light is much more likely to give a diffused wash of light onto a surface and is softer. One big problem with some direct light fittings is that they cause glare, where light from the lamp shines directly into

OPPOSITE: LED recessed uplights highlight the frames of the high windows.

A living room with downlights for washing the walls, and table lamps and pendants for ambient light. (Photo: Marcus Steffen)

the human eye. This causes the eye's pupil to constantly dilate and contract to compensate for this large burst of light against a background of much lower light emission in the general room. Exposure to this for an extended period of time can cause exhaustion and headaches as the brain constantly tries to adjust for the contrasting light levels. One solution to this is to use fittings with anti-glare baffles or louvres, reducing the angle at which the lamp can be seen. Generally these anti-glare features do not affect the light output of the light fittings.

Indirect light by its nature does not produce glare. It relies on washing light onto a surface which then reflects the light back into a space. It is used in a huge variety of ways, from washing whole walls to lighting up bookshelves and cupboards. Indirect light is a good source to use when a relaxed atmosphere is required, since the lack of glare and the evenness of the light output reduces strain on the eyes, and makes the room appear 'softer'. This is an ideal choice of light for bedrooms and living rooms, and anywhere where a relaxed atmosphere is desired.

Caution must be used with indirect light, since too much can create a bland and flat space with no character. It is

Plaster wall lights provide a wash of light onto the daybed as well as indirect light onto the ceiling. (Photo: Mr Resistor)

better to light a few surfaces than all of them, leaving some in shadow to provide contrast and interest. This is especially relevant with ceilings built with coffers to conceal an uplighting element. While there is light all around, the lower part of the ceiling is in shadow, throwing the centre into contrast and preventing it becoming bland.

Another complication with indirect light is that the surface it is illuminating will affect the light in the room far more. Dark surfaces do not reflect much light, meaning either a much more powerful light source will need to be used, or other lighting will need to be added into the room. Brightly col-

oured surfaces inject that colour into the space, colouring everything with a shade of the colour on the wall. This can ruin the effect of feature walls, and create an uncomfortable room with too many overpowering colours. Gloss surfaces reflect light but do not create a soft light, since they act like a mirror. This means there is a much higher chance of direct glare, and the light fittings will also be visible rather than concealed. The ideal surface for reflecting indirect light is a matt one in a light neutral tone. This is not to say that it should never be done in a different way, but a matt, neutral surface gives the softest light with maximum brightness.

The ceiling in this room was dropped in the centre to allow space for ventilation pipes, and the resulting change in height has been turned into a lighting feature with indirect lighting. (Photo: Mr Resistor)

The Colour of Light

The colour of light is essential to lighting in a home, and is a very misunderstood area. In very general terms there are cold colours and warm colours. Cold colours appear with more blue inside them, whereas warm colours have more yellow. In fact, as well as the cold/warm variation, there is also a shift between red and green, which has become much more prevalent with the increased use of fluorescents and LEDs on the market. While this can cause a problem, well made fluo-

rescent and LED lamps should generally achieve good whites with very small green or red shifts. Variations in cold and warm colours are much more common since both are desired in different areas of the industry. Daylight (very cold) is used a lot in office spaces to create a natural effect, whereas very warm colours are used in homes. It is important to remember that natural daylight is very cold. It is only the quantity of daylight which offsets this. Colder colours look good when used at high lighting levels, whereas warm colours work better with low levels of light. Cooler colours can be used in areas such

An indirect wash of light from a fluorescent lamp in daylight (6500K) white. (Photo: Mr Resistor)

An indirect wash of light from a fluorescent lamp in interna (2700K) white. (Photo: Mr Resistor)

as bathrooms and kitchens, which are generally the brightest areas in a home, while warm colours are ideal for bedrooms and living rooms.

When deciding whether to use warm or cool light, the colour scheme used in the room should be considered. Colder colours, such as blues, greens and greys, become much more vibrant under cooler colours. Oranges, reds and yellows, as well as creams and browns, show up much better under warm colours. In some cases it may be that the material is either extremely warm or cool, and this needs to be countered. A good example of this is gold. If a lot of the interior is gold or orange, then cooler colours can control this, turning it into a champagne colour instead. If very strong colours are being used, it is worth doing tests before the final installation. If there is a mix, or a decision cannot be made, always err on the side of warmer colours in residential use.

USES OF LIGHT

General Light

The purpose of lighting in general is to give enough light so that the main purpose of the room is fulfilled for the majority of the time. Enough light needs to be provided to carry out day-to-day tasks. This does not mean that it needs to be evenly lit, or have extremely bright light all the time. A common mistake is to put a large number of light fittings in a property under the illusion that they are needed to provide extremely bright light. General light is about providing sufficient light for the purpose of a room. The purpose of a kitchen and a bedroom differ greatly, and so do their requirements for general light. To continue this example, a kitchen needs to have bright light since numerous detailed tasks are carried out

A living and dining space lit with central chandeliers, complemented with additional general lighting from recessed downlights. (Photo: Mr Resistor)

there, as well as numerous other jobs, such as reading recipes and perhaps children doing their homework. In a bedroom the requirements are far less. Normally only enough light is required for people to move around the bedroom, and there will be very few places that need high light levels. It is also not desirable to have an overly bright bedrooms since this can over-stimulate people just before they need to sleep.

The best way to approach the design of general lighting for a house is to analyse the layout of the whole space and identify the main areas. Spaces should be divided into areas that see frequent use and those that are only occasionally used. For example, a kitchen is used for many hours during the day, whereas a guest bedroom or bathroom would only be used for a few weeks of the year. The purpose of the room

ILLUMINANCE LEVELS

The level of illuminance on a surface is measured in lux. This is the amount of light (lumens) over a given area. While this is not essential information when producing lighting designs for residential properties, it is helpful to know about lux levels and how bright they are. In the case of light fittings, especially spotlights, manufacturers often give a light cone diagram which will show the illuminance at the centre of the beam at different heights from the floor. This helps to give some guidance on what a lamp can achieve in comparison with other lights.

EXAMPLES OF DIFFERENT RECOMMENDED ILLUMINANCE LEVELS

This table shows different areas and guideline illuminance levels:

Kitchen – 300lux

Dining Room – 100–250lux

Living Room – 200lux

Bedroom – 150lux

Bathroom – 200–300lux

Hallway – 100–200lux

POSITIONING OF DOWNLIGHTS

A very common mistake made when positioning downlights within a ceiling is to make the spacing between each of the downlights and the walls of the room the same. Unfortunately, the light falling within the space is not going to be even since the outside of the room will be in darkness. When spacing downlights, it is best for the distance from the wall to be half the distance between the light fittings.

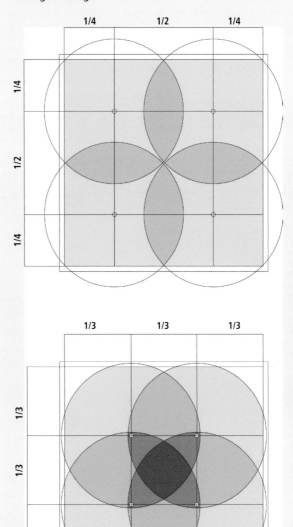

Diagram showing different spacings of downlights and how this affects the pattern of light. (Diagram: Marcus Steffen)

should also be taken into account, since some rooms require more light than others. This information provides guidance on how much general light to allow for, and the levels of light required. The CIBSE does provide some guidance on lighting for different areas, but unlike in commercial buildings, this is not a rule, and variations are very common and even encouraged. Finding a plan that works for an individual building is much more important.

A good way of achieving general light is to use distributed lighting across an area. Recessed downlights allow pools of light to be overlapped, giving good powerful light downwards onto surfaces, and they can be tailored to fit spaces. Powerful uplights on the walls can reflect light off a lightly coloured ceiling and back into the space. This has the benefit of providing an indirect light source, reducing glare. Care should be taken in large rooms when using wall lights since it the light will not normally reach to the centre of the room. Hang-

ing pendants or chandeliers are not usually a good source of general light. If one pendant is positioned in the centre of the room, then as a person moves around the room they will create shadows on the walls and floor, and this contrast of light and shadow moving around can be quite discomfiting. Since focus is normally directed across the centre of a space, it also means a person would be looking at the pendant frequently, and the glare can become quite irritating. Pendants and chandeliers can be used, but they work much better in conjunction with other forms of lighting to act more as a feature than a light source.

Task Lighting

Task lighting is light that is provided for particular tasks being done in a space. In any room there are normally areas that

A bedroom with two bedside lights providing task lighting for reading as well as ambient lighting. (Photo: Marcus Steffen)

Cool white light used in the under-cupboard and internal lighting to complement the monochrome finish in this kitchen. (Photo: Mr Resistor)

need a higher level of light due to the tasks being carried out there. Some examples are kitchen worktops needing extra light for when food is being prepared, while living rooms need extra light around seating areas for reading. Task lighting is essential for living in a space, but it also adds to the overall inviting feel and comfort of a home. It is important to have a good level of task lighting in all areas, and it is often best to start a design by considering where task lighting is required.

The light levels for task lighting need to be higher than those for general room lighting, so it is best to use light fittings that can produce a concentrated light over a specific area. Downlights and spotlights are excellent for task lighting, since the controlled beam angles found on halogens and LEDs allow the light to be focused onto the work surfaces and achieve a high illumination. These types of fittings are also available with options where the direction and tilt of the lamp can be varied, and this allows the light to be angled onto a work surface, even if it is not directly above it. They provide

an efficient way of creating task lighting in the areas where it is needed, without it spilling onto other areas. This saves energy, since light is not wasted on spaces that do not need it. Some halogen lamps (known as heat forward lamps in the industry) reflect the heat out into the room rather than back into the ceiling void. If these types are being used, then it is important to consider the heat build-up when arranging the task lighting. If a person is going to sit under one of these lamps for a long time, perhaps reading a book, then it may be worth considering other options, since the heat will become uncomfortable.

Pendants can be hung over an area which requires task lighting. This is particularly common over dining tables and kitchen islands. If a pendant is going to be used for task lighting, then it is important to make sure it provides enough light. Ideally the light will be directed downwards onto the surface, rather than being emitted all around. Pendants with shades, especially ones made of reflective material such as chrome or with a white paint finish, are best for focusing light downwards, and are ideal when used in groups over a large area.

When furniture is located above the surface requiring task lighting, such as wall cupboards above a kitchen worktop, then under-cupboard lighting is a fantastic option. There is a range of options for this, including strips and spots, but is important to consider how they will be installed and what level of light is required. There are many different fluorescent strips on the market, which produce high levels of light onto the work surface. The fluorescent tubes are also available in different colour whites, so if a cooler colour is needed, due to décor requirements, then it is possible to achieve this. It is very important that the light fitting is installed with a cover to protect the glass tube. Under-cupboard lights can be hit and broken, and if a fluorescent lamp shatters then there will be glass all over the work surface. Many fittings are available with polycarbonate covers which protect the tube and prevent it being broken.

LEDs provide an alternative to fluorescents for strip lighting. Although they are currently not as powerful as fluorescents, the technology is progressing all the time and LEDs will eventually overtake them for both light quality and output. LED strips are normally very small and easy to install under cupboards. Due to their nature of their construction, there is no glass, and the fittings are normally more durable than fluorescents. The light is also normally more focused onto the worktops due to LEDs having a beam angle of 120° or less. This can make them more efficient at lighting a worktop than a fluorescent, especially if they are mounted above a dark-finished surface. (Fluorescents lose light since they emit light

A wall light on either side of the mirror is used to give a balanced wash of light across the face. (Photo: Mr Resistor)

in a full 360°.) LEDs are also available in a wide variety of whites, and have very long lives, so do not need much maintenance.

No matter what strip light is used, certain provisions need to be made for them within the construction of the cupboards. Most strip light fittings are not particularly nice to look at, so should be concealed from direct view. This can be done in a number of ways. One of the simplest is to have a small pelmet on the front of the cupboards that conceals the lighting. This is very easy to construct and makes access and positioning of the light fittings very easy. Pelmets are normally found on more traditional styles of kitchen cupboard. In a very modern kitchen, especially where there are no trims or detailing on the cupboards, then a pelmet can look out of place. In this case the light strips can be recessed into the bottom panel of the cupboard. Fluorescent fittings are normally too large to accommodate this, but LEDs can be very shallow, as little as 6mm deep, so it is easy to router out a small channel to install them into. This will ensure that the line of the cupboard is not broken. Unfortunately, sometimes recessing even an LED strip is not possible, either because of the style of cupboard or because of the breaks between the units. There is one final option: the cupboards can be set off the wall, normally mounted on wooden battens. This can give the illusion of the cupboards floating above the work surfaces, but allows space for a small LED strip to be placed behind the cupboards to throw light downwards onto the work surface. There are two important considerations when using this method. The first is how the cupboards are seen from the room. If the sides of the cupboards are visible, then it will be possible to see the back of them, and this construction detail is unlikely to be flattering. An oversized end panel will be required to conceal it, and this can be difficult to obtain if an off-the-shelf kitchen unit has been used. The other consideration is the depth of the cupboards. Usually there is a work surface below them, and if the cupboards protrude too far out, then it will make this work surface awkward to use. The offset distance should be kept to a minimum, which means LEDs are normally the most convenient light source to use.

If strip lighting is not possible, for whatever reason, then spotlights could be used under a cupboard. Spotlights create pools of light along the work surface, and are normally spaced relative to the cupboard sizes. It is important to check the beam angle of under-cupboard spotlights, since they need to be positioned close enough together to ensure there are no shadows. Halogen spots are the most common. These

are made with a capsule lamp and a rudimentary metal or plastic reflector. They are neither efficient nor particularly good at lighting a work surface, but they are low cost, and the ones most kitchen manufacturers and installers choose. LEDs are becoming more common in under-cupboard spotlights as they become more efficient. These have the advantage of a long life and a wide spread of light if desired. Due to the construction of LEDs, they are also very durable, with no glass like halogens or fluorescents. They can be more sensitive to heat than halogens though, so they should not be placed above a cooker. Small fluorescent spotlights are also available. These produce a lot of light, but it is not normally directionally controlled since the reflectors necessary would be too bulky. They can be a low-cost but energy-efficient solution, however.

Mirrors used for applying make-up and shaving also require good task lighting. The classic Hollywood mirror design, with lamps all around the frame, is actually one of the best designs for mirror lighting. It is important to have the light coming from all directions, with an even level of light to ensure that no shadows are cast on the face. This can be done with strips around the sides of the mirror or behind frosted glass panels, or by having wall lights positioned on either side, or at top and bottom.

There are numerous other areas in a home that require task lighting. It is important to identify these and allow the correct lighting levels for them, since it can be very frustrating when a person is trying to work and there is not enough light. This can even become detrimental to their health, weakening their eyesight and causing extra stress and tiredness.

Ambient Lighting

If general lighting is the basic requirement, and task lighting the practical element, then ambient lighting is what gives a home its soul. This is where lighting can play such an important part in the mood and psyche of an occupant. Ambient lighting is what changes the lighting from a standard type to something amazing. It adds the warm, cosy environment that people desire within a home, making it a sanctuary from the world.

Ambient lighting is commonly brought into the home with decorative table and floor lamps, which create pools of light around them. Table lamps with shades create some of the best ambient light since there is very little glare. The light is spread up and down, providing some light reflected off the

Two bedside lights create pools of light beside the bed, providing practical reading light. (Photo: Mr Resistor)

SPACES WITH A LARGE AMOUNT OF GLASS

Glass is a difficult surface to work with when trying to light a space. Glass creates a mirror image of what is in the space, but does not reflect light back into the room. In rooms where most of the surfaces are glass, such as conservatories or glass house extensions, this can complicate the lighting design. It is worth remembering a couple of facts. First, it is going to be very difficult to get any soft, indirect light into the space. Since most of the surfaces are glass, the light will not be reflected back into the room, so direct light sources must be used. If there are any large, flat surfaces not made of glass, then these should be lit to reflect as much indirect light into the room as possible. Secondly, it should also be remembered that any light fittings will be visible in the reflections in the glass. Thus all the light fittings should be aesthetically pleasing when seen in the reflection. For example, if a light fitting is being hidden in the coving to wash a wall, and there is a glass skylight above, then the light fitting should look good enough to be viewed directly since it will be seen in the reflection in the skylight.

Glass at night appears as whatever surface is beyond it. This is normally black, since the external area will be in darkness. There will be very little indirect light since there are no surfaces to reflect light and this can result in a harsh and uncomfortable area. The best way to introduce a soft light is by creating lit surfaces on the shades of table and floor lamps. These create pools of soft light and generate good task lighting in localized areas. Window shading systems, such as blinds, curtains and shutters, turn the glass into a surface more like a painted wall, and allow more indirect light within the room.

SMOOTH AND ROUGH FINISHES

All surfaces reflect light to a certain degree. A very smooth surface will be highly reflective, and it is sometimes possible to see a partial reflection, almost like a mirror. In a building these surfaces may include those painted with a gloss paint and polished wooden floors. The opposite of this is a rough surface, which does not create a reflection. Such surfaces can include matt painted walls and rough stone floors.

It is important to know what finishes are present if indirect lighting is going to be used within a room. Most indirect lighting, such as LED strips, do not look attractive. LED strips have many little LEDs, whereas wall lights have linear lamps that are also best concealed. If they are lighting a smooth surface, then rather than seeing a wash of light, the actual light source may be visible in the reflection. This is very common in kitchens with glossy work surfaces, such as marble. Under-cupboard lights will be mirrored in the surface and become visible. In these cases the actual look of the light source needs to be considered since, despite being hidden from direct view, it will still be visible within the room.

Corner wall lights both accent the shape of the staircase and highlight the texture of the wallpaper. (Photo: Mr Resistor)

A niche containing a statue is lit with two small uplights, while the stairs are lit in a contrasting colour. (Photo: Mr Resistor)

ceiling and also a concentrated pool of light below. Indirect lighting is the key to creating good ambient light within a room. Anything that produces glare can make the lighting seem harsh, which is the opposite of what is desired.

To create a good ambience within a room, the lighting should be layered. Layering is combining different light sources to create a light texture across the room. If only one type of light is used, such as downlights, then the light only travels in one direction, in this case downwards. This creates shadows on the ceiling and the tops of the walls. By combining different types of lighting, such as downlights, table lamps and wall lights, the light will be spread across all the surfaces in the room. The key is to make sure the light is not spread too evenly. Without contrasting light levels, the space will look bland and flat. Using different lighting types creates varying light concentrations within the room, focusing on the features and creating texture within the space. The layering and texture create comfort and warmth within the room, without it being overpowering. Concealing and building-in lighting around the room creates soft lighting flowing in different directions and naturally producing contrast. If a linear strip of lighting is laid around the coving in a room, washing light onto the ceiling, then it naturally creates a line of contrast at the coving, and provides an interesting defining line. To create good ambient lighting this contrast is needed, but the shadows should not be stark. It is not desirable to sit in a large dark room with only a small table lamp giving a pool of light next to the occupant. The room should be lit pleasantly with the features highlighted and other areas dimmer. In this way an inviting atmosphere is created, rather than an oppressive one.

Effect Lighting

Effect lighting is used to create art and beauty within a space. It can be used for almost anything within a room: a crystal chandelier, coloured lighting or even a starlit sky on the ceiling. The effect should be a feature within the room, just as a piece of furniture is. If the effect is being created by a light fitting, such as crystals refracting the light and making patterns, then this is very much a subjective choice. The light fitting and its effect should be tailored to the design and architecture of the space. Sometimes it may be done by matching the décor to the fitting, but it could also be achieved by creating a juxtaposition with the interior and the features within. This will depend on the choice and taste of the interior designer

and will be different in every property. It is important not to place too many features within a room. If there are too many, then they will not be the focus of the room, and it will look overcrowded, bland and tasteless. In general, the old rule of less is more applies here, and choosing one or two effects is best. They must either be complementary, or must be controlled so that they do not clash. Scene-setting can be excellent for this, since these systems ensure that two lighting circuits are not switched on together. This way a colour change effect can be produced in a room for a fun party, but for something more sophisticated this could be switched off and the artwork within the room lit instead.

Effect lighting can also be used to highlight specific items within a room, such as artwork or sculpture, or even architectural features. No other feature in the room will stand out without the light in the room. Even if no decorative lighting is being installed, lighting is always needed to highlight the decorative features within the room. Doing this correctly can be difficult and requires thought and planning at the very beginning of the project. It is beneficial to have an idea at the start as to what the main features within each room will be. Sometimes it is not possible to know if there will be artwork or sculpture, or a piece of furniture in a certain place, but some preparation work can still be done. If there is a large empty wall, for example, then there is a good chance that a painting might be hung there. The same can be said for console tables and other pieces of furniture. With a little bit of planning, the common feature areas can be identified. One set of features that is always known about at the start of the project is the architecture. All architectural features will be planned at the start of the project, so it is easy to plan how to highlight them with lighting. If a beautiful staircase or bath is being installed, or perhaps ornate window or door frames, then these can all be highlighted to help show off the beauty of the building itself.

Lighting Artwork

Lighting artwork can be one of the most tricky areas of lighting design, but the basic principles are simple. The goal of lighting paintings and photographs is to place a brighter light onto the artworks than the surrounding areas so that they stand out. Even if the room is extremely bright, and the pictures are lit well to be viewed, if they are not brighter in contrast to the main environment then they will not become a feature. There are a number of different light fittings available specifically for lighting artwork.

A painting lit by two camera slot downlights. (Photo: Marcus Steffen)

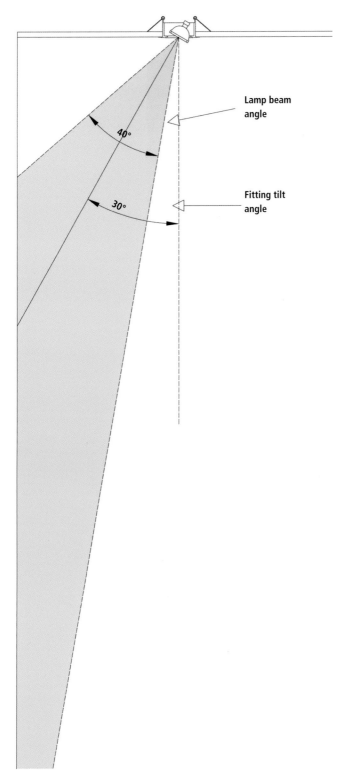

Lamp beam angle

40°

Fitting tilt angle

30°

Diagram showing how a downlight shines its light onto a piece of artwork, and how the beam of the lamp shows which section of the painting will be lit. (Photo: Marcus Steffen)

Picture lights are designed to light artwork. These are light fittings that are normally fixed to the wall and have a long tubular body that stretches across the body of the artwork, washing light down its surface. Unfortunately most so-called picture lights do a poor job of actually lighting artwork. The light is concentrated at the top of the painting or photograph and, unless it is very small (less than 40cm high), it will not be lit properly. Picture lights are really only suitable in a period property, where they fit in with the décor of the space.

Recessed downlights and spotlights use the same lamps and work in the same fashion when lighting artwork. They allow the placement of high levels of light onto the artwork, allowing it to stand out easily, and they bring out all the colours present in the artwork. The placement of the lights is important to ensure that the whole piece of artwork is lit, especially in rooms with low ceilings. The light fittings used should be adjustable so that the light can be targeted onto the artwork. The fittings should be placed close to the wall where the artwork is to be hung to ensure that it catches the maximum light. If the fittings are too far away, then it will not be possible to light the top of the painting. Using the tilt angle of the downlight, and the beam angle of the lamp, it should be possible to work out where the top of the beam will contact the wall, and this will define the distance that it should be placed from the artwork.

Framing projectors are the best way of lighting artwork. These fittings create a rectangle of light that can be projected onto the artwork, picking it out perfectly. Other light sources will be visible as an effect, but the framing projector just lights the artwork. The colours become more vivid and vibrant, making the artwork stand out against the background. If done well, it is not actually possible to tell that the paintings are lit by an external light source, and they seem to have an inner light source illuminating them. Unfortunately, framing projectors are very expensive, and so they are not normally used. If a piece of artwork is the highlight of a residence, then a framing projector should be seriously considered.

Lighting Sculpture

Lighting a piece of sculpture is a very different proposition from lighting a two-dimensional piece of artwork. With a flat canvas the aim is to light the entire area so that it is all visible. Due to the three-dimensional nature of sculpture, there is much more to do with the light. The aim is not to light all surfaces evenly, but to highlight the form and shape of the

A statue lit with a single downlight, creating a large contrast on the surface itself as well as with the surrounding area. (Photo: Marcus Steffen)

sculpture. The play of light and shadow define the sculpture and highlight its features.

Generally the best method of lighting a piece of sculpture is with a beam of light coming from a single direction. Most commonly this is a downlight casting a narrow beam of light onto the piece. This picks it out in exclusion of its surroundings, and creates a stark contrast between the upper and lower surfaces. The downlight should be placed above or slightly in front of the sculpture position, and should be an adjustable fitting. A narrow beam lamp, around 15°, is the best sort to pick out the artwork.

Another way of lighting sculpture is to have an uplight in front of the piece. This creates the opposite effect from the downlight, highlighting the lower surfaces but leaving the upper surfaces in shadow. It is important to position the uplight just in front of the sculpture so that it is caught by the beam of light. Ideally the fitting should be adjustable. This is

a very common method for lighting statues in outdoor locations, and often it is done with small spotlights rather than recessed uplights. It can also be a useful method if it is not possible to install a spotlight or downlight due to the ceiling construction.

Floor-mounted Uplights

Floor-mounted uplights are, by their nature, effect lights. By inverting the direction in which light normally travels, they create an effect that is different from the other lighting in the room, making it stand out. Most uplights have controlled beams of light, up to 60° wide. If the beam is wider than that, or if it has a frosted glass in front of the lamp, then it gives just a very soft glow, rather than a wash of light, and will be more of a marker light than a dramatic effect light.

The key to using recessed uplights is to ensure that the light

Recessed uplights wash up a wall behind a bath. (Photo: Mr Resistor)

falls on a surface so that it is seen. If an uplight is placed in an open space, then all that will be visible is a spot on the ceiling and a very bright point of light in the floor. The uplight should be placed close to a surface so that the effect and shape of the beam of light is seen. Uplights can be used to highlight the architecture of a space, such as door and window frames, fireplaces and pillars. They can also be used to create patterning and interest on otherwise plain walls. The controlled beam of light creates a contrast between dark and light, making this effect very dramatic.

Uplights on the floor have one major drawback, which is glare. The uplight is positioned low down but this falls into the eye line of the viewer much more than a downlight would. It is also more difficult to fit uplights with anti-glare systems, although some uplights come with a baffle or diffuser that helps reduce glare. When choosing where to place an uplight, the general line of sight of the room's occupants should be considered. If the occupant is going to be looking down in a particular area, such as at a table, then it may be a bad idea to place an uplight next to it. Uplights should always be in addition to other lighting within the space. There should be general lighting so that there is an option to switch off the uplighting in a room.

Star Ceilings

A star ceiling can be a major feature in a room. It can be done on a small scale, such as a few stars above a bed, to a very large one such as a ceiling painted like the sky, which can then turn into a starry night sky with all the constellations. Fibre optics are used to create this effect since there can be hundreds of points of light for a low cost per point. LEDs can be used, but generally they are too powerful and the glare within a room can be too much for the space.

The installation of fibre optics can be quite complicated and should be planned from an early stage. The best method is to have access from above so that small holes can be drilled and the fibres fed through them into the main room. If there is no access from above, then careful discussion with the builder will elicit the best way for the

A star ceiling created with fibre optics. (Photo: Mr Resistor)

A bath surrounded with colour-changing LED uplights. (Photo: Mr Resistor)

fibres to be fed through the ceiling. One of the most popular methods is to use a stretched fabric ceiling. This consists of a frame with a light fabric stretched across it. The fibres can be pulled through the fabric before it is stretched, and will be hidden behind the fabric when it is in position. Alternatively a suspended panel could contain the star ceiling, creating a section of false ceiling. The panel can be raised and suspended once the fibres are installed and the surfaces are painted.

Colour-changing Lighting

Colour-changing lighting is normally created using RGB (Red, Green and Blue) LED fittings. These are available in an array of forms, from spotlights to strips. Unfortunately, the name is a misnomer, since the colours generally do not change all the time. Rather, the ability to change the colour allows the creation of almost any colour that is desired to change the mood and feel within a room. With the addition of white light, pastel colours can also be created. It should be remembered that colour from light is additive. This means that if all three colours are turned on, then it will create white light. Darker shades of colours can only be created by the lack of light. This means that it is not possible to create very dark hues without reducing the brightness in the room to below practical levels.

Colour-change lighting is a very decisive product in lighting. While some love the ability to choose whatever colour they want within a room, others feel that it can be kitsch and unfashionable. As with most design products, it is not the product itself but rather the way it is used that is important. Used in moderation, it can be an amazing way of lighting a space, and can change the entire mood and feel of a room. Used carelessly, it can create a clashing colour scheme that assaults the senses and makes it quite unpleasant to occupy the space. It is almost always sensible to have only one colour at any time. If there are different colour-change fittings in the room, then they should be synchronized so that they always match. It is also best not to use colour-change lighting within a room that already contains strong colours in the decoration. These coloured finishes will clash with and distort the coloured light in the space.

CHAPTER 5

THE HEART OF THE HOME: THE KITCHEN

Good lighting in a kitchen is one of the most important parts of lighting design, and it can dramatically affect how people use the area. The old saying that the kitchen is the heart of the home is very true, and the lives of many individuals and families are focused around it. Often it is incorporated into an open plan living area, which may include a space for dining, but it is essential to make sure the lighting is tailored for the kitchen area itself. It is just as important, if not more so, to get the lighting right in a small galley kitchen, since space is normally at a premium and it must be as functional as possible.

When approaching a kitchen lighting design, it is useful to start with the task lighting before the general lighting. There are many work areas in a kitchen that require bright light, and sometimes the task lighting can also provide the general light in the kitchen. If the general light is done first, followed by the task lighting, then it may be that either too many light fittings are put into the design, or a compromise is made on where the task lighting can be used.

LIGHTING KITCHEN SURFACES

The kitchen surfaces are where all the main work takes place. Whether it is a marble worktop or a butcher's block counter,

OPPOSITE: Pendants over the kitchen counter provide good task lighting as well as a feature within the space.

people will be chopping vegetables and meat, cleaning up spills and dealing with hot pans while they cook. Working in poor light can turn the task of cooking dinner from a joy into a chore, with the chef becoming tired and frustrated. Similarly, no one likes washing up and cleaning, but in poor light these jobs are a nightmare. Poor lighting means that people cannot properly see what they are doing, and at worst this could result in accidents – such as fingers getting cut while vegetables are being chopped. This is why getting the lighting right in the kitchen is probably the most important area for lighting designers.

Downlights are one of the most popular ways of providing task lighting in a kitchen, with good reason. They give powerful, controlled light down onto the work surfaces, and it is easy to place them on the ceiling where they are needed, rather than relying on cupboards or extractor hoods for placement. They are also discreet and do not get in the way. When it comes to maintenance, they will not get as dirty as other lights mounted closer to the work surface. It is often best to purchase adjustable downlights. These do not cost much more than fixed ones, but they allow the light to be angled onto the work surface, meaning that there is more flexibility in the placement of the light fittings. In most ceilings there will be joists that may prevent downlights being placed in certain positions, but with adjustable downlights that can be angled onto the work surface this is not an issue, and if you need to move them by 20cm in one direction it will probably not matter. Always ask the electrician to check the final placement of the downlights before cutting the holes, since it is not possible to go back once this is done.

It is also popular to place pendants over islands and peninsula units in kitchens. These can provide a fantastic focal point for the interior design, as well as providing good, practical

A kitchen with trimless double downlights and linear lighting built into the skylight and cupboards. (Photo: Mr Resistor)

A triple downlight above the island provides general light on the work surface. (Photo: Mr Resistor)

light for the work surface. The pendants can be hung quite low so as to create a good focus of light into the workspace, without much spilling into the surrounding areas. This helps to increase the light levels on these critical areas, as well as making them stand out from the surrounding areas with higher light levels. Care should be taken when deciding which light fittings to use. Generally it is good to choose a fitting that is easy to clean, since more dirt and grease are generated in a kitchen than in other areas in the house. It is also worth considering what views are available in the room. If a large fitting is chosen, it may block the view to an outside space through large doors or windows, thus spoiling the flow of the space through the room. If there is a view that needs to be visible, then glass or chrome fittings that will reflect the light or allow it to pass through are good choices. Smaller fittings can be used in groups to great effect; for example, positioning three pendants above a long island can have a dramatic impact.

Under-cupboard Task Lighting

Where cupboards are located above the work surfaces, lighting can be fixed underneath them to provide some task lighting. These lights are normally built into the furniture or concealed by a pelmet at the front of the cupboard. Many kitchen suppliers provide under-cupboard lighting, though it should always be checked with regard to the quality and type of light fittings and lamps supplied. There are generally three main types of light available for under-cupboard lighting: low-voltage halogen, fluorescent and LED.

Choosing the correct white light is very important to making the kitchen work surface look good. Generally in a home it is safer to stick to the warmer colours, with a temperature of between 2700K and 3000K. This works in some kitchens, but due to the fact that kitchens can come in all colours and finishes, it is important to tailor the colour to the kitchen. In a monochrome colour scheme of black and white, a warm light will make it feel dirty. A colder white, say 4000–6500K, will make it feel clean and crisp, and maintain the monochrome look. In contrast, traditional wooden cabinets and worktops do not take a cold white well, making it look clinical and losing a lot of the warmth in the wood. Using a warm white in these areas gives a feeling of cosiness and makes it an inviting space to be in. Bright colours should be considered carefully in the overall scheme. If the colours have a warm base, then a warmer white will generally work, whereas a cold colour such as blue generally works better with cooler whites.

Care should be taken over metallic colours. With golds, a warm white can actually end up producing a yellow or amber light in the room, so it might be worth using a slightly cooler white, between 3500 and 4000K. This produces a more champagne-coloured light in the room, which can soften the vibrancy of the gold. If a silver is being used, then it should

Plinth, under-cupboard and above-cupboard lighting provide a contrast in colours, creating interest in this simple kitchen. (Photo: Mr Resistor)

be examined closely. Different stainless steels and nickel finishes normally have a colour undertone, such as blue, green or yellow. This should be taken into account to avoid a clash with the colour of the light. A warm light applied to a green-tinted nickel can end up looking a sickly brown, which is not normally desirable. It is best to test samples under different lights to see what works best.

Low-voltage halogen is the most common type, with small, round or triangular fittings using a halogen capsule lamp. These can either be recessed into the base of the cupboard units, or mounted on the surface. The light fittings normally incorporate a rudimentary reflector to bounce as much light as possible onto the work surface. Low-voltage halogens require a transformer, which is generally located on top of the cupboard. It might be possible to run more than one from a transformer, but care should be taken with regard to positioning since generally transformers cannot be connected to the light fittings by a cable longer than 2 metres. Access to the transformers should be considered if this kind of lighting is to be used in a design. There is a large range of these types of fittings on the market, but generally they all produce the same pool of light under the fitting. Normally one is needed per 600mm cupboard to produce a good light underneath.

Two adjustable-height pendants provide task lighting for the island, while under-cupboard lighting illuminates the other work surfaces. (Design by Leigh Everett. Photo: Mr Resistor)

There are a number of disadvantages with the halogen lights. The first is power consumption. Like all halogens, the majority of the power input into the light fitting is emitted as heat. Along with the low light output, the heat also creates a second problem, in that most of the heat is radiated up into the cupboards, meaning that there is normally a hot spot over the fitting, which can cause items stored in the cupboards to heat up. If any food stuffs in this area are susceptible to spoiling, the halogen lights will cause them to age faster. Another disadvantage of the halogen lamps is the short life-span of the lamps. Generally they range from 1,000 to 2,000 hours. This requires repeated replacement, incurring extra cost.

Fluorescent strip lights are ideal under-cupboard lights. They come in a variety of lengths and fit under most cupboards, and they produce a high output of light. Different diameter tubes are available. The most common ones are the T5 (16mm) and T8 (26mm). Generally T8 tubes are not used for under-cupboard lights due to their size, but the T5 is suitable. There are also smaller ones, going down to 10mm diameter. Care should be taken to ensure that a ready supply of replacement tubes is available, since if a new lamp cannot be found then the lighting will most likely not be used, resulting in a degree of frustration. Fluorescent tubes require a ballast to work. This is like a transformer, though it works differently from the ones used on halogen lamps. As standard, fluorescent ballasts are not dimmable, and if dimmable ones are purchased, then they will not be compatible with standard dimmers. They generally dim using SwitchDIM, 0–10V or DALI. All these methods require extra wiring. It is worth considering a light fitting that has a cover. In a kitchen grease and dirt from cooking and preparing food can get everywhere, and if there is a cover, then the light fitting can be simply wiped down. With a cover there is also far less chance of accidentally knocking the fluorescent tube and perhaps breaking it, getting glass and other materials everywhere. Fluorescent lamps come in a variety of different colours of white, enabling the light to be tailored to the colour of the kitchen and highlight a strong colour scheme. It is important to note this colour in any design schedule to ensure that the correct lamps and replacements are purchased. Multiple fluorescent fittings with different colour lamps will clash, causing the kitchen to look like a run-down shop interior.

LED strips provide an energy-efficient solution to under-cupboard lighting, with low power consumption and good light output. Due to their life-span, it is possible to have light fittings that will outlast the life of the kitchen itself. This means that the kitchen work surfaces will be lit correctly the entire time. As with fluorescents, there is a range of whites available. Great care should be taken when selecting a colour. Most companies label their LED products across a range of whites from 2700 to 6500K. Because of this, they label 2700–4000K as 'warm white', but this is not the case. Most people recognize warm white as 2700–3200K. Anything between 3200 and 3800K is considered more of a neutral white, while anything above 3800K is cool white. When choosing LED strips, make sure that the colour temperature is listed, since this is a much better way of determining exactly what colour you will get.

LED strips generally require an LED driver to power them. This is similar to the low-voltage halogen transformer, though the type of voltage and current they output will be different. It is important to match the correct driver to the LED strip being used, and normally they should be purchased from the same company so that there is little risk of this being incorrect. LED drivers can normally be positioned further away than transformers for low-voltage halogen lamps, and the top of the kitchen cupboards is usually a useful and accessible location. If the LEDs are to be dimmable, a dimmable driver must also be purchased as it will not normally come as standard, and will most likely use a different dimming method from those found in standard wall dimmers. It will probably use a 0–10V or DALI dimming method, like the fluorescent fittings, and so special wiring will be required. It is best to work out what is available in the switching system that is being used, and then find a driver that works with that dimming system.

LEDs should be fitted inside some sort of body that is easy to clean, and there should be no exposed parts that can make maintenance difficult. Rather than LED strips, LED spotlights can also be used. These are normally compact and come in a variety of light outputs and colours. Some look more stylish, so if the fittings are exposed they are worth considering, though the light produced is not generally as practical as that from the strips. Strips give a good, even wash of light along a work surface, and do not produce shadows. Spots give concentrated pools of light, and if an item such as a mixer is positioned under one, it may create shadows on that part of the work surface.

Colour-changing LED strips, which can be used to produce most colours, are also available. These normally use combined red, green and blue LEDs to generate almost any colour in the spectrum. This can look fantastic when a particular colour is

An LED colour-changing strip mounted under a plinth highlights the floor and 'floats' the island on light. (Design by Leigh Everett. Photo: Mr Resistor)

used in the kitchen design, but it should be noted that RGB lights do not give a good white light and are not a substitute for white under-cupboard task lighting. Some LED strips are available with red, green, blue and white LEDs (RGBW), and these can provide a solution to providing both good colour and a practical white light. Again, the white colour temperature should be checked to ensure it is the correct one to match the colour scheme of the kitchen. RGB and RGBW systems require special controllers and wiring, and their requirements should be checked with the supplier. This should be done at an early stage to ensure that the correct wiring is installed, rather than at the second fix stage when the

goods are purchased and there is no chance to correct the wiring.

There are other products which can be used for under-cupboard lighting, but they are generally not suitable:

Architectural incandescent tubes are long glass tubes with a filament inside. They are generally fragile, have extremely short lives and are very power hungry. They are very rarely used now, but were common in the past, so it may be that a project already has these installed.

Cold cathode, or neon, tubes. These are glass tubes custom made and filled with a neon gas. Due to their fragility, and the fact that they are non-replaceable without considerable expense, it is not a good idea to have these as under-cupboard lighting.

GENERAL LIGHTING

Creating a general light inside a kitchen is essential for almost any home. The kitchen is the heart of the home, and it is important to have good lighting where a large amount of time is spent. The task lighting in the kitchen will also provide a large amount of general light in the room. Starting with the task lighting design before the general lighting layout will help prevent the space becoming over-lit and reduce the number of redundant fittings. Once the task lighting is done, it should be possible to see where dark areas still exist. Care should be taken not just to put light in each space on the plan. For example, in a kitchen with cupboards and work spaces around the outside, and an empty space in the centre, there is no reason to produce the same amount of light in this unused space. As long as there is some ambient light in this centre space, so as not to have a very large contrast between light and shadow, it should be adequate. Having the cupboards and work surfaces lit also helps to focus attention on these areas, making sure they are the focal point of the kitchen, rather than the whole room being bland and blending into the background due to being over-lit.

If task lighting is already providing most of the light required, then it may be worth using other lighting systems to provide an ambient light level while not being visible within the space. An excellent way of doing this is to have uplighting from the tops of the kitchen cupboards. Most kitchen cupboards do not reach to the ceiling, and strips placed along the tops of the units will reflect the light off the ceiling and down into the kitchen space. This produces a good base level of light, while the task lighting provides higher levels where it is needed. With uplighting, there is an option to turn off the downlights and pendants to create a softer, indirect light source, which could provide an excellent ambience for eating or relaxing. This can also be a way to provide a good late-night light, since the glare is low. There are a few options in fittings. Fluorescents provide high levels of light with a low cost. They come in various lengths, though they may not fit perfectly on top of the units. LED strips provide a good, even light, though care should be taken to ensure the LED strip is powerful enough to provide ambient light within the room as well as being the correct colour. The actual colour should be checked, since the definition of 'warm white' within the lighting industry varies wildly. Most LED strips can be cut at certain points along their length, and these cut points are generally in quite small increments. This means it is possible to obtain a length that fits neatly on top of the cupboards. The third option is cold cathode strips, sometimes known as neon lighting. These are custom made and so should fit perfectly, and can even be shaped to fit curved cupboards. This is the most expensive solution, though in special situations it is worth it; for example, in a kitchen with unusually curved cupboards, it might be the only way to produce an even uplighting. They can be problematic to work with though, and if they get broken they will need to be remade.

It is worth considering how these lights will be cleaned. Dust and grease gather on the tops of the cupboards and they will need cleaning at some point. The light fittings should ideally be fitted with some sort of cover so as to make it easy to run a cloth over them and keep them clean. Covers are available for both fluorescents and LED strips, though cold cathode fittings can be problematic.

AMBIENT AND EFFECT LIGHTING

The kitchen is a fantastic place to play with different lighting effects. It is easy to make a standard kitchen look amazing if a little thought and consideration are put into interesting lighting. This can really make a difference, and it does not need to be hugely expensive to achieve a good result.

The uplighting effects detailed above are concerned with how to use uplighting to create general light, but it is also good for creating interesting features and effects. A soft, warm white glow can help turn a kitchen into a cosy and inviting space, and is an especially good choice for open plan spaces. A coloured light strip could be used to create a sense of drama and fun. Care should be taken in choosing the colour, since it must not clash with the colours present in the kitchen. There are coloured sleeves available for fluorescents, as well as LED strips in a variety of colours. To take it one step further, a colour-changing LED strip could be used, providing an almost limitless selection of colours. With colour-changing LEDs it is important to remember that while they are capable of producing fade and strobing effects, this is not their main purpose. They are best used to allow a large colour palette, so that different ones can be selected at different times to suit a

Under-counter strips make the island a feature, while an uplight highlights the entrance. (Photo: Marcus Steffen)

person's mood. Having a small selection of favourite colours would be the best possible use.

As well as uplighting, lighting can be added to different areas to give soft indirect lights. By placing a lighting strip under a plinth or a breakfast bar, a wash of light is created onto the floor. This can serve as both a good ambient light as well as a late night guide light, allowing someone to get a drink of water without turning on all the lights in the kitchen. The best lighting for this is an LED strip, since they are very small, making them easy to fit under the plinth or breakfast bar. As well as being too large, fluorescents also use fragile glass tubes, which could be easily damaged by being knocked. Even when using LED strips, it is best to either recess them or place them in a protective channel. It is very important to consider the surface onto which this light will fall. If it is a gloss or satin surface (such as polished stone or varnished wood), then it will be possible to see the light fitting itself, rather than just a soft warm glow on the floor. If possible, then, a matt surface should be lit. If this is not the case, then the chosen light fittings need to both look good and give a continuous light. Seeing lots of little spots from LEDs is not very nice, but a continuous light will create a line of light on the floor, giving an interesting effect. Normally this would require some sort of diffuser to be placed in front of the LED strip, blending out the spots of light.

Fluorescent strips with a sky blue sleeve flood the ceiling with blue light. (Photo: Mr Resistor)

Warm light is mounted above the cupboards, and contrasts with the cool light lighting through the glass splashback. (Photo: Mr Resistor)

Vaulted Ceilings in Kitchens

Vaulted ceilings can be a big issue when lighting kitchens. It is normally difficult to recess spotlights into the ceiling itself, both because of the type of construction and because the ceiling is much higher than normal, so other alternatives need to be considered. Remember that it is important to produce a good light on the work surfaces, as well as providing sufficient ambient light inside the room. If there are beams traversing the room, then surface-mounted spotlights could be fitted onto them, angled to light the work surfaces. Sometimes even this is not possible, either because there are no beams,

or because they are in the wrong positions to provide good lighting onto the work surfaces. In this case, the most must be made of under-cupboard lighting to light the work surfaces. Other alternatives are to have hanging lights over islands or work surfaces without cupboards above, or wall lights positioned around the sides that throw light downwards onto the work surfaces.

Producing ambient light is also essential to the creation of a lighting design for rooms with unusual ceilings. Without a soft light in a high-ceilinged room there will be a much higher chance of dark shadows being created. The combination of light and shadow is essential to a good lighting design, but having too much of one or the other creates an uncomfortable space. Vaulted ceilings can often be left completely in shadow, creating a black void above people. This can be oppressive and very off-putting since a cavernous space is created. At night this can make the occupants feel as if they are in a large hall rather than in a warm, cosy kitchen, sheltering from the night outside. A dark vaulted ceiling is never desirable, so it is a good idea to provide some uplighting into this space. As well as producing an indirect light source bringing ambient light into the room, it also highlights an important architectural feature in the room. Small floodlights around the sides of the space, angled up towards the ceiling, will help highlight and wash it. Anti-glare shields, such as barn door flaps, should be used to ensure that no uncomfortable direct light is emitted. Strip lighting positioned on top of the beams or cupboards in the space can also provide uplighting into the ceiling, both utilizing the architectural features of the room and highlighting them by the contrast of the lighting. Small spotlights can also be used. These will not wash across the whole ceiling, but rather create beams of light onto it. This method can be used to accent vertical beams, and is an especially good method for rooms with very old structures, such as barn and church conversions. It is worth considering all of these in combination, on separate switching circuits, to completely change the atmosphere and decoration of the ceiling.

CONTROLS

Kitchens rely on separate practical lighting circuits to be used to their best potential. If the kitchen is not in an open plan area, and is not used for dining as well, then it may not be necessary to dim, though this is always desirable. It is worth having the different areas of light controlled separately. Having the under-cupboard lights on a circuit that is different from the task lighting over the island, and then the plinth lighting on its own as well, will allow the lighting to be put to different uses. This means that only the necessary lights are on at any one time, saving energy.

If the number of circuits rises above three, then it is worth considering a scene-setting system. This enables the control of all the circuits onto a few basic scenes, which ensures that only the lighting which is needed is used. The most common are a bright scene, a serving scene and a night-time scene. The bright scene is for general use, such as cooking or work-

ing, and will have the general and task lighting on, but the effect lights may be left off. The serving scene is for when the kitchen is in use but is likely to be frequently left, such as during dinner or a party. The under-cupboard and other task lighting will be on, but the general lighting will be dimmed down, and plinth lighting and other effects may be on. The night-time scene is used for the evening when the kitchen is not in use. People may want to come into the kitchen to find drinks and snacks, but it is not worth having all the lights on. Just the under-cupboard, island or plinth lights are left on to provide a small amount of light. There could, of course, be more scenes than this, such as ones incorporating colour-change uplights on top of the cupboards or other effect lightings in the space, but these three are the most common.

If the kitchen is in an open plan space then it is almost always best to use a scene-setting system. Most open plan spaces have many circuits to help control where the light is used. A large bank of dimmer switches is normally an eyesore, and is unlikely to be used correctly. It is much more likely that the occupants will come in and turn on everything, since it takes too much time to tailor the lighting to a particular use of the room. This wastes a lot of energy, and the room will end up looking bland and uninteresting since the whole area is bathed in light, with no complementary light and shadow in the space. With everything lit, nothing stands out as a feature, so the island and units will be lost against the wash of light. A scene-setting system can make all the difference to this, allowing control over the different areas, with between one and three scenes for each 'room'. This makes controlling the light much more efficient and prevents lights being turned on needlessly, saving electricity. When dealing with kitchens in open plan spaces, it is worth considering where transitions are made between rooms. While it is always desirable to have control from the main entrance, the light will also need to be changed when going from cooking to eating. It is best to have an extra switch between the kitchen and dining areas so that this can be done easily, rather than having to go back to the main entrance.

It is also worth giving extra consideration to how under-cupboard lighting is switched. Many of the light fittings on the market have the option of integrated switches within their bodies. This can be an easy option to operate them, but it is not always very convenient. If there are many fittings they will all need to be switched on and off separately, which is a chore, and will ruin the effect of all the work surfaces being lit together. Even if they are centrally switched in addition to their integrated switches it can be troublesome, and if one or two have been turned off then it will look as if a few of the lamps have broken and not been replaced. It is best to have a switch that operates them all together. It is good to have one of these by the entrance into the kitchen, but it is also worth installing one next to the kitchen surface, especially if the surfaces are on the other side of the room from the entrance. This way, when a person wants to pre-pare food or drinks, they can walk up to the counter and just turn the under-cupboard lighting on, rather than having to walk over to the switch at the entrance and back again. This switch may be located on the underside of the cupboards, but it could also be installed on the splashback. Sometimes a different finish of switch will be required from the rest of the house due to being on the splashback, so this should be considered when specifying which one to use.

CHAPTER 6

LUXURY AND STYLE: THE BATHROOM

The bathroom is tied with the kitchen in its need for good quality lighting. Whereas food and drink is prepared in the kitchen, the home owners themselves are prepared in the bathroom. Whether readying yourself in the morning for a long day in the office, getting ready to go out for a night on the town, or just preparing to go to bed – at all times good lighting in the bathroom is essential. Along with practical uses, the bathroom is also a place to relax and unwind after a long day, letting go of the stress of the world and finding an inner peace. These multiple uses of the bathroom mean that the lighting must be flexible to suit any situation, and it should be possible to change the mood of the lighting to fit the mood of the user.

As well as the different functions of a bathroom, there is also an almost infinite number of ways in which a bathroom can be designed and built. It is one of the areas where the design can be anything, from traditional to brutal minimalist, and from large, palatial spaces to compact, efficient shower rooms. On top of the differing styles, there are safety considerations, including the waterproofing of light fittings and protection against electrical shocks. These safety requirements limit the types of fittings that can be used, adding to the complexity

OPPOSITE: An LED strip set into the counter provides lighting onto the glass and mirror, while recessed uplights behind the bath highlight the frames of the windows.

This bathroom uses recessed downlights for general and task lighting, as well as LED RGB downlights for effect lighting. (Photo: Mr Resistor)

of the design of the lighting. Despite all these complications, achieving good lighting inside a bathroom is still reasonably simple, and can be done like other rooms. It just requires a little bit more thought and planning.

SAFETY REGULATIONS AND WATERPROOFING

There are a number of requirements for waterproofing and safety features for light fittings in bathrooms. A qualified electrician should ALWAYS be consulted when choosing the light fittings and designing the lighting. At the time of writing (2013), this book refers to the 17th edition IET electrical installation standards, BS7671. Before beginning a design, it is essential to check the latest regulations and make sure the lighting design complies with them. There are two considerations for safety when choosing light fittings to work in a bathroom: the voltage on which they work and the IP rating of the light fitting.

Voltage

The voltage of the fitting is very important. If the voltage is high, and there is an electrical fault resulting in the live wires touching the casing, the result of contact with a person can be a large electric shock, resulting in injury or even death. As standard in the United Kingdom the domestic 'mains' voltage is 230V AC, although this can vary between 220V and 240V. This is a hazardous voltage, hence the large number of protective measures both installers and manufacturers take. In a bathroom, where water is more likely to penetrate a defective fitting, potentially creating a link between the electrical contacts and the body of the fitting, or a body of water, it is important to reduce the voltage to safe levels. Safety Extra Low Voltage (SELV) has a voltage of no more than 12V AC, or 30V DC. Even if a bridge is made by the water, and a person comes into contact with it, there is no chance of electric shock. It is even possible to touch the wires of a SELV fitting and not be shocked.

IP Rating

The second safety measure involves the waterproofing of the light fittings themselves. This is quantified using a rating system called the Ingress Protection (IP) rating. The IP rating consists of two numbers, with the first number ranging from 0 to 6, and the second ranging from 0 to 8. It is a common mistake to read both numbers, so that an IP rating of 45 is 'forty-five'. In fact, the two numbers are not related, with the first number relating to the protection from ingress of solid objects, whereas the second number refers to the protection from ingress of liquid objects. In the bathroom only the second number is relevant.

Bathroom Zones

A bathroom is broken up into different areas, or zones, with different safety requirements for each zone. There are three zones which are relevant to light fittings in the bathroom.

Zone 0 refers to the interior of a bath or shower tray, or a certain floor area extending from the shower outlet or drain in wet rooms. All fittings in Zone 0 must be SELV and have an IP rating of at least IP*7.

Zone 1 refers to the area above Zone 0 to a height of 2.25m. All fittings in Zone 1 must be SELV and have an IP rating of at least IP*4.

Zone 2 refers to an area extending 60cm horizontally from Zone 1, and also up to a height of 2.25m. All fittings in zone 0 must have an IP rating of at least IP*4.

In Zones 1 and 2, it is sometimes a requirement to have fittings rated IP*5, but this is only if the space is to be cleaned using water jets, as in commercial baths and showers.

In addition to the requirements for light fittings in the bathroom, switches must all be SELV inside a bathroom. There is no allowance for mains voltage switches in a bathroom, except for pull cord switches. Normally the light switches must be located outside the bathroom to comply with the regulations. This can cause problems if scene-setting, or mood lighting is to be used, though there are alternatives that are acceptable within a bathroom space.

GENERAL LIGHTING

Achieving a good general light in a bathroom is key, and this must be done correctly during construction, since it is not possible to go back later and alter it. In other rooms extra lights such as table and floor lamps can be added to boost

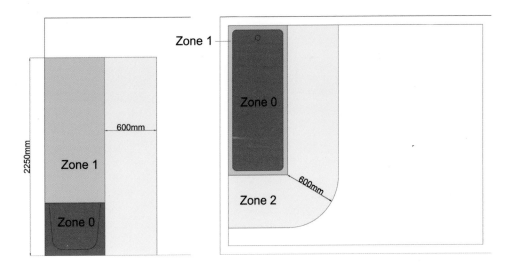

Bathroom zones around a bath. (Diagram: Marcus Steffen)

Bathroom zones around a shower with a tray. (Diagram: Marcus Steffen)

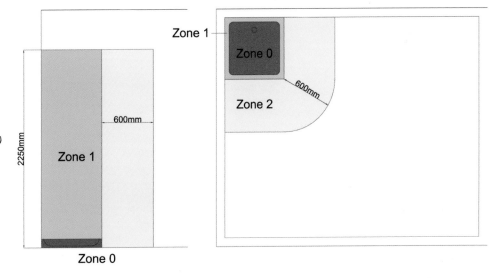

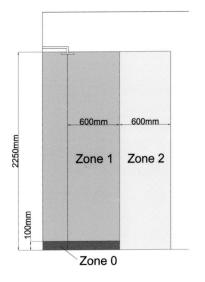

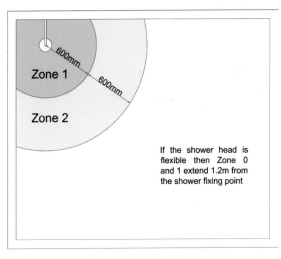

If the shower head is flexible then Zone 0 and 1 extend 1.2m from the shower fixing point

Bathroom zones around a shower without a tray, such as a wetroom. (Diagram: Marcus Steffen)

A fluorescent strip under the mirror helps eliminate shadows on the face when combined with downlights above. (Photo: Mr Resistor)

the light levels, but in the bathroom this is not possible. There will be no plug sockets in the bathroom (if there were, they would represent a huge safety hazard). Due to the restriction of waterproof requirements, the types of light fitting that can be used is drastically reduced. It is essential that the correct light fittings are purchased for the bathroom, and it is always a good idea to consult an electrician regarding the chosen fittings to ensure that they are satisfactory.

One conventional method is to use a surface-mounted fitting in the centre of the room, which is normally some sort of waterproofed dome or disc housing one or two lamps. This should be easy to install and gives an overall light to the room. Unfortunately, they normally do not emit enough light, and can create both shadows when someone uses the room, and a bland, flat light within the space. It is much better to have multiple light sources within the space to better balance the light and give a higher light level.

Recessed downlights, set inside the ceiling, allow light to be placed where it is needed, giving a good general light and also a focused light over sinks and showers. A range of different styles of fittings are available in suitable IP ratings, meaning there will probably be one to fit the design of the bathroom. Normally there are several focal points in a bathroom, such as a shower, shelves or sink area, and having downlights around these areas means there will be practical task lighting as well as good general light. In a bathroom good bright light is normally best, so sometimes wide angle lamps (45° and 60° beam angles) are used. Alternatively either lamps or fittings with frosted glass can be used to diffuse the light across the space. This is good for bathrooms, since a bright atmosphere is normally wanted.

Sometimes it is not possible to recess downlights, normally due to the construction of the ceiling. Since a centre light as described above is not desirable, alternatives must be found. There are some surface-mounted adjustable spotlights available that have the necessary IP rating for use within the bathroom. Almost always these will be mains voltage, so they are not suitable for Zone 1, but they could be used in the surrounding areas to provide a focused and powerful light that will produce a similar effect to recessed downlights.

One alternative to the direct lighting discussed above would be to use indirect lighting from hidden locations, giving a softer effect overall, and providing a light source that can be turned into an ambient light when relaxing in the bathroom. These indirect light sources could be built in around the room, generally around the perimeter of a dropped ceiling. It is important to be aware of where the bathroom zones

lie to ensure that the correct light fittings are used. Normally there are two options available: LED strips and fluorescents. If a waterproof fluorescent can be found, then this is a good option, since they have a high light output, providing the good light level required. Alternatively LED strips can generally be found in waterproof versions, and are normally of a much more compact size. It might be necessary to layer two or even three LED strips together to provide a high enough light level for general light. To find out how much is required, it is important to check the lumen output values of these LED strips and compare them with other similar lighting products, since there are a huge number available. If a dropped ceiling is not possible, there are other ways of building in indirect lighting. Furniture in the room, such as mirrors, cupboards and niches, can all play host to indirect lighting with some clever construction.

Lighting for Mirrors

Mirrors are very important in the bathroom. If the lighting is poor, then people will not be able to see themselves properly, and tasks such as applying make-up and shaving will become more difficult and frustrating. If the light quality is insufficient, then colours do not show up properly, and if the light level is too low then details cannot be seen. It is important to get the balance of the light correct in relation to the rest of the room. If the light level at the mirror is less than in the surrounding area, then even if it is powerful enough, it will make the face look darker compared with the background. The eyes adjust to the light level in the room, so if the main room is much brighter than the rest of the space then the brain will see the face as the darkest part.

When thinking about mirrors, it is helpful to imagine the classic Hollywood make-up mirror, with round lamps all the way around the perimeter of the mirror frame. These are normally incandescent lamps, known for their top colour rendering index, with a slight bias towards warm colours. The key to this design, and any design for a mirror, is to have light coming from all directions. Light travels in a straight line, so it is logical to imagine that if light only comes from one direction, shadows will be cast by objects blocking that light. With the classic Hollywood mirror design, the lamps are placed all around and emit light in all directions. This provides a good, even light onto the face of the viewer.

Unfortunately, the design of the Hollywood mirror is now under threat because of the disappearance of incandescent

Wall lights on either side of the mirror give an even wash of light onto the face. (Photo: Marcus Steffen)

lamps, but the principles of its design are as true as they ever were. When considering the lighting for a mirror, it should be made so that there is light coming from all around the mirror, or at least from four points. This light should be balanced in brightness, and needs to be powerful to ensure a good contrast with the rest of the room. A good colour rendering index is important too, since having poor quality light is going to be detrimental here.

A common way of lighting a mirror and sink area is to place a number of downlights above the mirror, generally two per sink unit, with the intention of lighting the face from two sides. Unfortunately this does not produce a very good light, since all the light comes from above, and it does not give an even light across the face. This results in shadows under the chin, nose, eyes and cheekbones, and distorts make-up since the balance in shade cannot be found. If no other alternative is available, and downlights must be used, it is best to position them as close to the mirror as possible, giving the best angle at which to wash light onto the face. Diffused light is best, such as frosted glass lamps or fittings, since this spreads the light more evenly and helps stop shadows. An alternative method is to use adjustable downlights positioned further out but angled towards the mirror so that the light bounces off the mirror and onto the face. While in principle this does provide a better solution, there are a number of practical problems with this method. The first is that there are not many adjustable downlights available with an appropriate IP rating, and this will limit the choice of fitting. The other issue is that

LED strips under the cupboard and sink provide an excellent night-light. (Photo: Marcus Steffen)

normally a fitting must be used that can tilt up to 45°–70°, and these are quite rare. If a high enough angle fitting cannot be used, then all the downlight will do is light the top of the head of the person in front of the mirror, and provide no light onto their face. It is best to consider downlights as good lighting for a sink area, which is important, rather than as mirror lighting.

Wall lights are a very common option for lighting around a mirror. Again, the principle of having an even light all around the mirror is important, and it should be of good quality. It is not unusual to have a strip above a mirror, but this is not a good way of lighting, for the reasons given above for downlights. It is much better to have lights either on both sides, or above and below a mirror. Having a wall light on either side provides light from two directions, balancing the lighting and reducing shadows on the face. The style of the light fitting is important. Small spotlights are not sufficient, since they produce beams of light and an unevenness that is not helpful. Ordinary lamps in fittings do suffer from having a point of light emission, resulting in shadows. If a fitting can be obtained that has a diffuser, this will help to spread the light more evenly, and give a better wash of light onto the face. A lot of light fittings for use around a mirror will be fitted with a glass or plastic cover to provide waterproofing, and these covers are normally frosted, providing the necessary diffusion. Another good option is to have a fluorescent wall light, especially one with a linear fluorescent tube. These provide a distributed line of light, which emits light evenly along the entire length. Long strip fittings on either side can produce an effect extremely similar to that of an ideal mirror light. It is very important to purchase high quality fluorescent tubes, preferably from one of the high end ranges made by a major manufacturer. Look for a high colour rendering index, rather than the standard tubes on the market. There is also a range of colours available, but generally it is best to stick to 3000–4000K and a colour rendering index in the 90s.

Lighting can be hidden behind the mirror itself, and produce light through the mirror surface. Mirrors are generally made from glass with a mirror backing applied to it. This means that it is possible to leave a section of the glass uncovered, allowing light to flow through it. These sections are normally frosted as well, camouflaging the lighting behind, and giving the illusion of glowing panels of light. Generally fluorescent or LED strips are hidden behind, to emit light through these frosted glass areas, giving illumination. Since the pattern of glass frosting can be anything from two lines to a circle or oval, it can create a very effective light for applying

make-up. It is important to make sure the lighting behind the mirror is powerful enough, though, since the glass reduces the light emitted by 50 per cent or more. The other difficulty that can occur when doing this sort of design is providing access for maintenance. Eventually the fluorescent lamps or LED strips will fail and need to be replaced. There must be some way of gaining access to them, and this may require the removal of the entire mirror. If this cannot be easily done, perhaps because of the size of the mirror or its fixing, then it is not a viable solution. It is possible, when constructing the wall where the mirror is to be mounted, to allow for special fixings so that the mirror can be pulled off when access is needed. For a mirror that runs across the full width of the wall, it is possible to have separate strips with the frosted glass. In this case, those smaller strips can be removed, but the large sections of the mirror remain permanently fixed. With careful planning and design, it is possible to design in these details so that they both provide good illumination and practical maintenance. There are mirrors available on the market with built-in lighting. These are easy to mount and come as a complete package, sometimes with storage and shaver sockets built in, but they are available only in fixed sizes and they may not suit all rooms. The quality of the light must be checked before purchasing, since they vary wildly across the market.

In more modern bathroom designs, it is sometimes not possible to have wall lights, either because they do not fit with the style of the bathroom, or because there is no wall to fit them onto, such as when a mirror is made to the full width of the wall. In these cases it is worth investigating built-in solutions, where the light source can be hidden inside the construction of the wall or mirror. The options for this are unlimited, and depend on the design of the bathroom and its furniture. It is common to have a floating mirror, with the strips placed behind the outer edge, so that light washes around from all sides. This relies on good reflections from surrounding surfaces, so it is not advisable in rooms with dark finishes. A good way of creating reflective surfaces to light back onto the face is to create a recess in the wall that is larger than the mirror itself. The mirror is mounted in line with the wall, reducing the intrusion into the room and giving cleaner lines. The recess can be finished in a light colour to provide a good reflection, and the light strips can be hidden behind the mirror itself. The finish around the mirror should be non-reflective, such as a matt paint or tile, since otherwise the light strips will be visible. High brightness fittings should be used here, since the light is reliant on reflecting off the surrounding surfaces, and this reduces the light output.

AMBIENT LIGHTING

Creating an atmosphere in a bathroom is very important if it is going to be used for relaxation. If it is just a small shower room, it may be the case that a good, bright light is all that is required, but for a bigger room, perhaps with a large bath where a person can relax and wash away the stress of the daily grind, then ambient lighting is essential. While relaxing in the bathtub it is unlikely that someone is going to do anything requiring a bright light level, so it needs to be possible to turn the lights down and create a soft, warm glow. Generally it is worth splitting the lighting in the bathroom onto different switches so that this is easier to do. For example, the main downlights could be turned off, or dimmed down, in favour of having indirect lighting in niches and under the bath. It is generally not a good idea to have bright downlights directly above the bath, since the light will shine directly into the face of someone lying back in the bath, and this glare is not pleasant. If lights have to go above the bath, it is best either to place them very close to the wall with no frosted glass, or to have adjustable fittings, which can be aimed at the wall to give a wash of light, reducing glare.

Since it is not possible to place table or floor lamps inside the bathroom, other methods need to be used to give soft light in this area. Indirect lighting is key, since this provides little or no glare, and helps create that relaxed atmosphere. Building in this lighting to the natural architectural features of the room will help reduce its impact on the visual lines of the room, while enhancing the mood through the soft light they emit. Prime locations for these lights are on top of furniture, such as mirror cabinets, and at low level, for example under the sink, or a bath trim. Placing an LED strip under a floating sink unit will wash light across the floor and reflect upwards into the room, both highlighting the floating sink feature and giving a soft glow. LED strips can also be hidden under a lip in the bath panel at low level. If a space is left at the bottom then it will wash light across the floor.

LEDs in the niches provide an excellent contrast with the colour-washed walls, while the LED strip in front of the bath gives an excellent wash of light across the floor. (Photo: Mr Resistor)

Another good location for lighting in the bathroom is in small niches around the room. Normally storage space is at a premium in a bathroom, so recesses formed into the walls near the bath and shower provide places to store items, as well as a good area to conceal some lighting. Positioning small LED downlights inside these alcoves, or a strip running along the back, will give a good light, but contain it to the niche itself. A light located in the niche will light up all the surfaces within the niche, but not the surrounding surfaces. This creates a nice contrast between light and dark, and makes the niche a feature within the room, since it will be brighter than the surrounding surfaces. When building the lights into the niches, special consideration must be given to the construction. It is likely that the niches will be tiled, so it must be

possible to drill a hole through them for downlights, or have a recessed channel to conceal an LED strip at the back of it.

Uplighting from the floor is a good option. Normally uplights located inside the floor have a problem with glare, since people look down more than they look up. When a person is in the bath, however, their line of sight will be upwards, so any glare from the uplighting will be hidden. If the bath is built in, then it may be worth locating the uplights in the corners, where a natural cavity occurs. If it is a free-standing bath, the lights could be located behind the bath in the floor, washing light up the walls. They can even be used to wash onto the bath itself, which is especially effective if the bath has a textured finish. It is worth remembering that the point of the uplight is to wash light onto a surface. Do not

The bath is highlighted with small recessed uplights, while the sink has excellent task illumination, with light from above and below.
(Photo: Mr Resistor)

simply place them in random locations where the light effect is not going to be seen, as then they will be little more than marker lights, rather than providing a good visual impact for the bathroom.

Lighting at Night

A bathroom is a room that is visited at all hours. During the night, in the darkness, the eye becomes much more accustomed to low light levels. If the lights have to be turned on, then this will ruin a person's night vision, leaving them to stumble back to bed. A good feature to have in a bathroom is a light with a low light output, which can be used as a night-light. This can be any sort of light, but generally it is LED, since there are low output LEDs available, whereas incandescents and fluorescents all come in very high output lamps, even at the lowest level. Ideally the light source will produce an indirect light, washing across the floor to enable the user to see where they are going, but not giving any direct light, which could be irritating.

Low-level LED wall lights are a good option for night lights. The light emitted is normally directed downwards, and will wash across the floor, meaning reduced glare. They are generally recessed into the wall, rendering them unobtrusive, and they can have an exceptionally low power requirement, generally between 1W and 3W. Another alternative is to place an LED strip under a floating sink, or into a recessed channel low in the bathroom, providing a wash across the floor. These lights are much more dependent on how the bathroom is to be designed, but since they are hidden there is no possibility they will clash with the style and design of the bathroom.

With regard to controlling the night-lights in a bathroom, it is important to ensure that the main lights are not accidentally switched on instead of the night-lights. One option is to make sure the switches are separate on the wall, so that they cannot be mixed up. Alternatively a different kind of switch could be used on the same plate, with dimmers for the main lights, and an on/off for the night-lights. One good option is to have the night-light linked to a motion sensor within the room, which turns the light on when someone walks into the room, meaning no switches are required. Passive Infra-red (PIR) sensors are available in a number of styles, and ceiling-recessed ones can be used, keeping them discreet within a room. Each sensor will only cover a certain area, so it is worth checking with the manufacturer to see whether two or more sensors are required to cover the whole bathroom. Walls and glass block detection by PIR sensors, so it is important to position the sensors where they can pick up motion around the entire room. PIR sensors stay active as long as they detect movement, but after the movement has stopped they have a small internal timer that counts down to zero, at which point they switch the lights off. If any movement is detected within this countdown period, the sensor will reset and start again once the movement has stopped. Normally PIR sensors have settings that enable the time delay to be adjusted. Some also have adjustable settings for the light level at which they turn on. This means that during the day the lights will not come on when they detect movement, but they will activate when there is no natural light.

Highlighting Textures and Finishes

Perhaps more than any other area in the home, bathrooms are the most likely to have heavily textured walls, or floors finished in interesting colours and materials. Whether they are polished marble or rough-hewn stone, special consideration must be given to the lighting. Ideally, these finishes will be highlighted to form a feature within the bathroom. Lighting up these surfaces is normally a simple affair, but care must be taken to ensure the light effects match the material. For example, a material with a lot of colour will not benefit from being washed with a colour-changing light, since most of the effect will be lost. If there is a heavy texture to the surface, such as offset stone in an alternating pattern, it is worth positioning some downlights to wash down the surface. This will produce a light grazing effect, with only the tops of the stone lit, and the undersides in shadow. It is important to get the downlights close to the wall, so that the light travels at a sharp angle down the wall. If the lights are too far from the wall, the lower parts of the stone will be lit, and this will ruin the contrast of light and dark.

If the surface is a glossy material, such as polished marble or travertine, then it will be important to ensure that there are no poor reflections from this surface. If a light is too far away then it will be reflected as a point of light in the surface, and will reflect back into a person's eyes, creating glare and making the bathroom uncomfortable. Ideally lights should be placed close to the surface to wash down or up it, and they should be fitted with anti-glare technology, such as a black baffle. Another alternative is to create a light effect that looks good when reflected. A good example of this is creating a blended line of light along the whole surface of the wall. If this

Uplights behind the sink highlight the beautiful material it is formed from. (Photo: Mr Resistor)

is reflected then it will appear as a simple line of light, with little or no glare. Another alternative is to use a beautiful light fitting that will appear for a second time when reflected. This works on mirrored surfaces to some effect, though there is less reason to highlight a mirrored surface, since it is merely showing a reflection of what is present in the room. With mirrored walls it is better to light the other walls and objects in the room, since these highlighted features will then be reflected in the mirrored wall.

Creating Drama

Sometimes a bathroom is not only a place to relax, but also a showpiece for the home. Creating dramatic effects can wow

visitors to the bathroom. It is ideal to create a dramatic effect in a room that is not used for long periods of time, such as a guest bathroom. It is still important to provide good general light as well as dramatic lighting, since sometimes the room will need to be cleaned, and this will require a good light level. Dramatic lighting is normally achieved by creating a large contrast between light and shadow. By having only feature areas lit, and all other areas left in darkness, these feature areas stand out even more.

Narrow-beam lamps in downlights can focus light onto particular areas, creating small pools of light, without much spilling out around the room. They can be used above sinks and other furniture to highlight them and should be fitted with anti-glare attachments such as black baffles, since glare inside a dark area can ruin the effect. Having small lights inside

LED crystals above a shower create a focal point within this bathroom. (Photo: Mr Resistor)

niches can add to the dramatic effect, since the niche itself will help control the light and prevent it spilling into the rest of the bathroom, increasing the contrast and dramatic effect.

Recessed uplights in the floor of the bathroom can be used to throw light up walls and create an inverted lighting effect. This can look very dramatic since the contrast of the light on the lower parts of the walls and the light level on the floor is very high. It is important to remember that recessed floor uplights are not used to light the floor itself. The light travels out from the uplight into the top of the room before reflecting back down to hit the floor. Recessed uplights are in fact the worst type of fitting for lighting the floor itself. The positioning of the uplights should take into account the surfaces that the light will fall onto. As opposed to downlights, which are

used to put a certain amount of light onto a floor across a room for general light, recessed floor uplights are rarely used for putting an even light across a ceiling. Their main purpose is to wash walls with light and highlight architectural features in the room.

It is normally a good idea to place uplights evenly along long walls, so that a balanced pattern of light is produced. Placing them in corners can help draw the eye to the extent of the room, making it feel larger, and also framing the walls bordering those corners. If there is a boxed-out section in the wall due to pipe work, then generally a natural alcove will be formed on either side of this. If it is finished well, with uplights placed in the corners of these alcoves, it can turn a functional structural element into a defining feature in the room, while

A stone bath uplit with Swarovski Crystal recessed LED uplights, creating a pattern of light on the textured surface. (Photo: Mr Resistor)

not actually being visible. Since the uplights are placed in the alcoves, the face of the bulkhead is in a contrasting shadow, and will not draw the eye as much as the bulkhead.

Uplights can also be placed under a free-standing bath, to draw attention to its construction and make it the centrepiece of the room. This can create the effect of a warm glow around the bathtub itself, with light reflecting off the surface and onto the floor. It is important to check the finish of the surface of the bath though, since if it is poorly finished the light will only exaggerate any flaws. High gloss finishes will show not the light but rather a reflection of the floor, so if uplights are to be used here, then the material finish and style of the fitting is very important. Rough stone finishes are the best for uplighting, since the effect shows off the texture very well.

If the bath is built into the space near a wall, then uplights could be cut into the corners around the bath, creating a soft uplighting effect for someone relaxing in the bathtub. It is important to use fittings that have a baffle or some other sort of anti-glare technology in this situation, since they will be very close to the user. The fittings should also have an IP*7 rating. Technically they will be in Zone 1, but there is a very strong possibility that they will be splashed with water, and if they are to last then the best protection should be used.

Uplights are one of the few options available to light bathrooms where the ceilings are sloped. This is very common in bathrooms built in loft extensions. Generally it is not possible to fit any ceiling lights, and waterproof wall lights will be needed. Generally wall lights are not SELV rated, so they cannot be fitted in Zone 1, and this can cause serious problems with producing light at the sloped end of the room. If no light is used in this sloped end, then an unbalanced feeling is created. The portion of the room with the sloped ceiling will feel dark and dingy, and this ruins the effect of warmth that most people want to achieve within a bathroom. Placing a line of downlights in the sloped portion of the room will wash light up onto the ceiling and reflect it around the space. This will reduce shadowing in the corners, and help to balance out the light levels.

SWITCHES AND CONTROLS FOR BATHROOMS

The regulations on switches in bathrooms are quite restrictive in the UK, and generally it is not possible to place a switch within the bathroom. This restriction exists so that there are no exposed 240V connections within the bathroom space. If water was to condense on a wall and run down into the back of a switch, it could cause a short circuit, or even an electric shock to someone who touched the switch. There are exceptions to this rule though.

It is possible to put a pull cord switch in a bathroom. The base of the pull cord switch, which is either surface-mounted or recessed into the ceiling, is where the electrical connection is placed. The only connection to the switch is through a pull cord, normally made of string, which engages the switch on the switch plate on the ceiling. The string ensures there is no possibility of an electrical connection being made between the user and the electrical switch itself. The switch is also mounted high up on the ceiling, meaning that there is a much lower chance of moisture penetrating the body, since the water cannot run down a surface and into the back of the switch. Pull cords are a rather outdated method of switching, and are generally used for very small bathrooms or in older properties where they already exist. In general they need more maintenance than conventional switches since the cord can break much more readily than a standard switch.

It is also possible to have SELV switches within a bathroom. These carry a much lower voltage than mains voltage switches, so even if contact is made with the electrical parts of the switch, there would be no risk of electric shock. SELV switches do not switch the mains power themselves, but send a signal to a control unit, which performs the electrical switching. Generally these sorts of switch are used in scene-setting

control systems, but it is possible to have just an on/off or dimming switch.

The final option is to use a radio control switch. This works in a similar way to the SELV switch, but uses a radio signal rather than a low voltage current linking the switch to the circuit controller. There are two parts to a system like this: the transmitter and the receiver. The transmitter is the switch on the wall, whereas the receiver is a relay or dimmer switch controlled by a radio receiver circuit. When a signal is transmitted from the switch, the receiver picks it up and tells the relay or dimmer switch to adjust its state. Transmitters are generally battery powered, and for use in the bathroom they must be. Radio switching can provide a lot of flexibility within a bathroom. It allows the switch to be placed on any surface, since no cables need to be run to it. For example, if a surface-mounted transmitter switch is used, then it could be fixed onto a glass panel and there would be no unsightly wires. It should be checked whether the switch itself is waterproof. While it will pose no danger if it gets wet, it may be damaged. It is best to locate it somewhere within the room where it is unlikely to be splashed or exposed to a lot of moisture.

The receiver must be placed outside the bathroom zones and in a secure location. Above the ceiling or in a cupboard outside the bathroom are the most common locations. As with all electrical equipment, it should be accessible for maintenance. Generally most radio control systems have a certain range, and this should be checked with the manufacturer. The structure of the building may affect this range, and in some cases can reduce it dramatically. Neither the receiver nor the transmitter should be placed inside a metal box, since this will prevent any signal being transmitted or received. If the walls in the building are very thick (approximately 600mm) and made of solid material, such as in very old cottages with solid stone walls, then this can also drastically reduce the range. Reinforced concrete can also be a problem since it has a steel wire structure running through it. This kind of material is used in blocks of flats, but it is rare to have walls constructed of reinforced concrete within an apartment. Newer styles of wall, such as stud partitions and brick, are normally fine.

If none of the above switch types is used, then the switch must be located outside the room. This will prevent any risk of electric shock, though it can make controlling the lighting within the room quite difficult. When choosing the lighting for a bathroom it is best to have good general light and also an ambient light for relaxing in the bath. Unfortunately the

EXTRACTOR FANS WITHIN THE BATHROOM

Extractor fans are not lighting, but they are normally linked to the lighting in the bathroom. Most bathrooms today are fitted with an extractor fan. As well as providing air circulation, they can also help prevent the development of damp problems and mould. The most common way of controlling an extractor fan is to have it switch on with the general lighting, and then have a timer to turn it off after the lights have been turned off. These timers are normally adjustable, allowing the time the fan remains on to be varied. Unfortunately it is not possible to dim the majority of the fans on the market, and since it is wired in with a lighting circuit, this will not be dimmable either. This is not ideal in larger bathrooms, though for small shower rooms it may not be a concern. While there is no solution with standard switches, scene-setting control systems can provide an alternative. Since the scene-setting allows the control of multiple circuits from one button, it is possible to wire the fan and lights separately. When the button is pressed to turn them on, it will turn on two separate circuits, and this enables the lighting to be dimmed.

Fans can also be controlled in other ways. Two popular options are to use either a humidity sensor or a PIR sensor. A humidity sensor is sensitive to moisture in the air, and will turn on once it exceeds a certain threshold. Once the moisture drops below the set level, the fan turns off. The threshold can normally be varied, though it will depend on the model of fan and sensor. This removes the fan totally from manual control, and it will always be ready to activate. A PIR sensor-controlled fan activates when it detects movement within its zone of control. If the movement stops, then a timer counts down and turns the fan off. This provides responsive control of the fan, while still allowing the lighting to be dimmed. Careful placement of the unit is important, since the sensor needs to cover the whole bathroom. In larger bathrooms this is not an ideal solution, since the sensor may not be capable of detecting a person on the other side of the room, and the fan will be turned off prematurely.

In some properties a centralized ventilation system is used. In this kind of system the fan is located in one position in the property, and pulls air through ducting, which is run to all the bathrooms and other areas in the house. The fan normally runs all the time, and provides extraction for all the bathrooms. This has two main advantages: the fan is not controlled by the light switches, and the whole system is much quieter, since the fan is located elsewhere.

general light is needed for getting ready to get in the bath, and then it needs to be changed to the ambient light. If the switch is located outside the bathroom, then this becomes awkward, though not impossible, especially if it is an en-suite bathroom, so there is less risk of being interrupted. Ideally dimmer switches will be used, since they allow for control over the brightness of the lighting and help create a relaxing atmosphere within the bathroom.

Scene-setting controls can be used in a bathroom to help control and set the mood of the room. They are not necessary in small shower rooms where only general lighting is needed, but in large bathrooms it can be a wonderful feature to change between bright light and a relaxed ambience at the touch of a button. When getting ready for a long bath, it will be necessary to have some general light in the space, but once in the bath a relaxed light is preferable. It is important to be able to change between these settings easily without leaving the bathroom. Using a system that has wireless or low-voltage switches that can be placed in the bathroom allows changes to be made very quickly and in the privacy of the bathroom. These switches should, however, be positioned away from the bath or shower, since, while they are not a danger, they may be damaged by water ingress.

There are generally three common scenes for a bathroom: a general scene, a relaxed scene and a night-time scene. The general scene will have most of the lighting on in the bathroom, giving the bright light needed for having a shower and putting on make-up. The relaxed scene is used when having a bath or getting ready for bed. It has a soft, ambient light, with the general and task lighting turned down. The night-time scene has the lowest level of light possible, and is used for visits in the middle of the night. The night-time setting will not startle people awake, and makes getting back to sleep much easier.

CHAPTER 7

COMFORT AND RELAXATION: THE LIVING ROOM

The living room is the area where families and friends gather to relax. Whether it is after a day of hard work or a dinner party, people gather in the living room to socialize and unwind. This space can be the centre of a party, an area to watch television or just a sofa where a couple can have a chat. The living room has a myriad uses, and so the lighting within this space must be flexible. There must be both a powerful general light and a soft ambient light for use late at night. Task lighting must also be considered, since there could be a number of different areas that need it, and each may require a different solution.

When planning the lighting for the living room, it is important to have some idea of the layout of the furniture. If this is not known, then the lighting can end up looking generic and bland, resulting in a lacklustre design. The more that is known about the layout and the use of the space, the more the light can be tailored to complement the space. Even if it is not finalized, it is normally possible to determine approximate positions of furniture such as the sofa and the television. It might be narrowed down to two different layouts, and with these there will be shared features such as side table positions and built-in furniture. By using this as a starting point, the lighting can be placed in complementary positions, and this in turn can lead to choices being made about the layout of the interior.

Within a living room almost any lighting tool can be used since the layout in this room is the most flexible in the whole home. Whereas a kitchen needs to have units stuck to walls, and bathrooms must have basins, bathtubs and showers, the living room can be laid out in almost any arrangement. The free-form nature of the living room is what makes it one of the most fun areas to work with, where creativity can run wild without it creating a nightmare to live in practically. The furniture in this space does not need to be practical, but just stylish and comfortable. The living room is the area where almost anyone can get involved in the interior design, since it will not require major building work to change. This extends to lighting, where any kind of light fitting can be incorporated into the design. It is an area where strange and wonderful designs of table and floor lamps can be used alongside unusual lighting effects from interesting pendants to downlights.

GENERAL LIGHTING

As with any room, general lighting is crucial to the lighting design. In a living room achieving general light can be done by almost any method. In a kitchen the general lighting comes from the task lighting above the work surfaces, and will necessarily be constrained by what fittings are able to produce this task lighting. In the living room almost any type of light fitting can be used to produce the general light. It may also be layered up from ambient and effect lighting, rather than simply using light fittings designed to give general light.

Lighting the sofa area

The sofa (or perhaps a collection of chairs) is one of the fea-

OPPOSITE: LED strip set into the cupboard top highlight the wall, while plaster wall lights provide general illumination.

COMFORT AND RELAXATION: THE LIVING ROOM 103

LED double downlights provide general light within this living room, while outdoor wall washers bring the courtyard into the space. (Photo: Mr Resistor)

A floor lamp provides excellent task lighting for this chair, as well as an ambient light within the room. (Photo: Marcus Steffen)

the surrounding space appear darker, making the rest of the room seem less inviting. If the light is too diffuse, then long periods of reading can result in tiredness.

The most common way to light a sofa is with a table or floor lamp at one or both ends. These lamps create pools of light for the areas where a person is most likely to sit, providing good task lighting for someone who is reading, but also introducing a soft ambient light into the room. If these lamps are dimmable, either through integral dimmers or via a circuit of 5A sockets, then the light they produce can be varied to match the current use of the room. 5A sockets also make controlling the table and floor lamps much more convenient because there will be just one switch to turn all of them on and off, rather than having to switch them individually.

Table and floor lamps come in an almost endless array of designs and functionalities, so it is important to find the right one to fit with the interior design and also to produce the correct light. It is always best to see the lamps in person before purchasing, since some have very little light output and are purely designed as decorative features. Becoming familiar with different styles of table and floor lamp will give a good idea of the light output that can be expected, and planning becomes easier if the light output is known beforehand. It is also important to provide some other source of light, even if it is only a central pendant, as if another person moves into the property, they may not have the right sort of lamps.

When changing the lamps of the table and floor lights it is important to observe any restrictions on wattage and lamp type. Shaded fittings have limits on the wattage of lamp that can be used due to the heat limits of the materials. In addition, it may be that a certain type of lamp has to be used. Fittings with integral dimmer switches may only be able to dim incandescent or halogen lamps, for instance. There may also be a transformer incorporated into the light fitting, and if the incorrect lamp is placed inside then this could fail. If the light fitting uses a fluorescent or LED lamp then it is possible that it has been designed to work solely with this specific type of lamp. For instance, if a floor lamp uses a 24W T5 fluorescent, which is 600mm, it will not be possible to change this for a 14W T5 fluorescent, even though it will fit. This is because of limits on the transformer or ballast within the light fitting.

One of the best ways of using floor and table lamps is for uplighting. From dedicated uplighters to simple shaded table lamps, there are many different styles available to wash light onto the ceiling. Some emit light both upwards and downwards, providing good task lighting, while others have adjustable heads that can be angled to give the best wash of light

tures that define a living room. This is where people spend the majority of their time within the living room, and will be one focus of the task lighting. In a kitchen a person moves around and utilizes most of the space, but in the living room a person is much more likely to remain in one small space, with different areas of the room occupying their attention. Focus may switch, for example, from the wall where the television is to the chair across the room when they are talking to a friend. It is also likely they will focus on the small space they are occupying, whether this is to read a book or use a computer. Providing a light source for the sofa can be quite difficult since it will need to adjust to what is going on in the room. If the light is too concentrated on the local area, then it will make

across a ceiling. A good uplight will have a high light output to compensate for the fact that it is reflecting light from the ceiling and then down into the room. They also need some sort of shade or anti-glare shield so that the light source is not visible. If a floor lamp is to be used in a room with a low ceiling, then its height should be adjustable. If the light output is too close to the ceiling, then there will not be enough space for the light to disperse and spread around the room. This will result in a hot spot of light on the ceiling, throwing the rest of the room into a darker contrasting shadow.

Bookcases and Shelving

Incorporating lighting into bookcases and shelves is a great way of creating an ambient light and turning a piece of furniture into a feature. Even if the furniture is not being specifically made for the building, it is still possible to add lighting effects to existing pieces. If the lighting is built in, the light fittings will not take up any space within the room, and will sometimes even reduce the wiring that is needed. The majority of the lighting ideas mentioned here deal with built-in furniture, but it is possible to apply these ideas to shop-bought furniture as well.

If lighting is planned for furniture, then a little preparation work is needed before installation. The cables must be provided to the correct locations to make sure the lighting within the furniture can be connected up. A bookcase is quite simple, since the cable just needs to be behind it. Shelving can be more complicated. If a frame is to be installed, then the cable can be brought to this frame, and a cavity can be allowed within it to run the cables to the shelves. If floating shelves are being installed, then the cable will need to be fixed at exactly the right height to line up with each shelf. This requires careful planning and accurate drawings to ensure it is placed correctly. The floating shelves also need to accommodate the wiring connections and any transformers, as well as concealing any cabling connected to the lighting itself. This can be quite complex, depending on the lighting being fixed to the shelf. For example, if recessed spotlights are to be used, then there must be a cavity to allow the cable to reach each spotlight, and the connections must be accessible for when replacements are required. While most of these allowances for cable can be designed into the shelves, a certain mini-

LED strips behind the wine rack highlight the bottles, making the rack a feature in the room. (Photo: Mr Resistor)

mum size of shelf will be needed to accommodate them. If the floating shelves are too narrow, then it may not be possible to build in lighting. If the wiring has been done for them, then this will need to be removed from the wall, causing extra building work, so it is worth considering if it is going to be possible to fit the lighting into the shelving before the first fix wiring takes place.

Most lighting installed into bookcases and shelves requires some sort of transformer. The maximum distance between the transformer and the lamps themselves varies depending on the type of lighting that is used and the manufacturer's equipment specification. If the transformer is too far away then generally the light output will be reduced, and the cable or lamps could be damaged. The transformer must also be accessible for maintenance and replacement when necessary.

Shelf Spotlights

Spotlights are simple to use; they can be placed on the underside of shelves, regularly spaced to create pools of light on the shelf below. The positioning of spotlights is important, and will be affected by what is being displayed on the shelf.

If there are to be books on the shelves, then the spotlights need to be placed towards the front of the shelf, so that they can wash light down the spines of the books. If they are too far back, then only the tops of the books will be lit. The shelf must have sufficient depth to accommodate this spacing; there is no point in installing spotlights on a shelf where the books are at the edge themselves. Spotlights are much more suitable for lighting small objects displayed on a shelf. One spotlight can be allowed per item, and will create a pool of light to highlight it. This will help draw attention to these items by making them brighter than the surrounding area. If only a few items are being lit, then a spotlight could be allowed for each. If there are many items, then it is better to have the spotlights spaced evenly so that the whole shelf is washed in light. This means that the whole shelf becomes a feature, rather than having one or two focal points along its length. Adjustable spotlights are not normally necessary for this kind of display lighting since the items being lit will be directly below the light. If adjustable spots are used, then the pattern they create should be planned in advance. If one of them is angled to the left and the rest to the right, then the light patterns will look disorganized and the effect will

Here the shelves have been floated off the wall, with rope lights placed behind them to create a silhouette effect. (Photo: Mr Resistor)

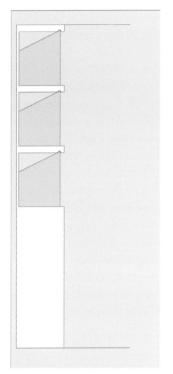

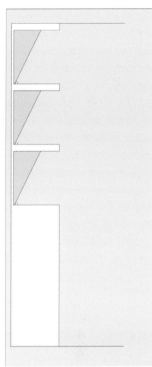

An LED strip recessed into the underside of the shelf at the front. (Diagram: Marcus Steffen)

An LED strip recessed into the top side of the shelf at the front. (Diagram: Marcus Steffen)

An LED strip recessed into the underside of the shelf at the back. (Diagram: Marcus Steffen)

An LED strip recessed into the top side of the shelf at the back with a lip to prevent it being covered up. (Diagram: Marcus Steffen)

be reduced. Ideally there should be symmetry in the patterning as long as there is symmetry in the furniture the fittings are being built into. For a group of floating shelves in a random pattern, then having different light directions may be suitable.

Shelf Light Strips

Light strips produce a wash of light along their length, rather than just a focused pool of light, and thus often blend in better with the architecture of the space, highlighting the forms used within the furniture rather than an individual piece. Light strips can be used for display lighting, but they work by drawing attention to the whole piece of furniture and what is on it, rather than just focusing on the objects themselves. Light strips are normally concealed within the furniture, hidden either in built-in details or by the body of the lights themselves. When installed, they should give a continuous line of light. If the line is broken at certain points without good reason, such as a vertical support, then it will break the

illusion of the light being linked to the form of the furniture. There is a range of different ways to mount the light strips on a shelf, and all have different purposes.

Positioning a light strip at the front of a shelf allows it to light the front surfaces of anything on the shelf. This is very good for books, since it will light up all the spines of the books, making them much more visible. The light strip can be angled to face backwards towards the wall, containing the light within the shelf. This makes it easier to hide the lighting because it is facing away from the rest of the room.

A light strip fixed at the back of a shelf will wash light across the back surface, whether it is part of the furniture or the wall itself. Any items on the shelves will be cast into shadow, creating silhouettes of them. This can be very effective, since it gives a hint of what is present on the shelves, while not revealing the items completely. This is especially good with books that are not very pretty to look at, but fill entire bookcases, such as textbooks for studying. By silhouetting them, they become a feature without being lit. Lighting can be used in this way both to make a feature of something, and to hide any flaws. More care is needed in how the light strip is built in when it is located at the back of the shelf. It is much more likely to be visible, especially if it is lighting upwards from the top surface of the shelf. The light strip can be recessed into the shelf, or a diffuser could be placed over it to create a line of light, rather than seeing individual points of light. The strip could also be angled backwards to light onto the wall, relying on the reflection from this surface to wash up the wall, though the distance it spreads up the back surface will be reduced. If the shelves are to be filled with books, then the strip could be mounted on the surface behind a small lip. This lip will act as a stop for the books to rest against, ensuring the strip is not covered up by them, which would create an irregular light effect.

Light strips can be used vertically or horizontally within shelving. Horizontal light strips illuminate each individual shelf, and throw the brightest light onto the surfaces. But there needs to be one strip per shelf so the cost can be high.

The wiring may be tricky, as the cables must run to each shelf. It is best, though, for silhouette effects, since each shelf needs to be lit evenly for this to work.

Vertical strips are normally located on either side of the bookcase, washing across the shelves. This can be much simpler than having individual shelves lit because the cables will naturally end at the top or bottom of the bookcase where it is easy to connect them. It is especially important to conceal the vertical strips. Unlike horizontal strips hidden under a shelf, it is much more likely that a vertical strip will be seen from the side when looking into a bookcase. Some bookcases have a lip on either side as part of the construction of the unit itself, and this provides a useful way to conceal the lighting. If there is no lip, then a recess can be formed in the side of the bookcase to conceal the strip. If this recess is set at a 90° angle, the light comes straight out onto the shelf, giving maximum projection of light across the bookcase. If the recess

An LED strip placed on either side of a bookcase, washing across the shelves. (Design by Chris Millard. Photo: Mr Resistor)

A strip mounted on either side at the front, hidden by a lip on the face of the furniture. (Diagram: Marcus Steffen)

A strip recessed into the sides at the front at a 45° angle to conceal it. (Diagram: Marcus Steffen)

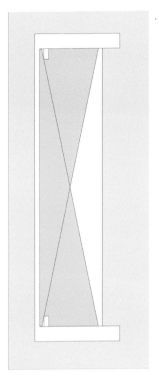

A strip at the back hidden by a lip in the furniture. (Diagram: Marcus Steffen)

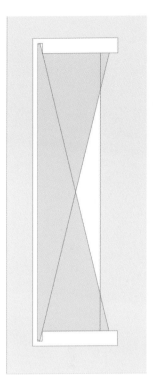

A strip hidden at the back by recessing on either side so that no detail can be seen. (Diagram: Marcus Steffen)

for the light strip is cut at a 45° angle facing the rear of the shelf, then it will be a lot less visible than one cut at 90°. The light will wash towards the back of the shelf, and the lip from the recess will conceal the light fitting itself. However, when the strip is angled in this way, the spread of light will not be as wide.

Vertical lighting strips are good for bookcases that are not too wide, or have multiple dividers. If the bookcase is wide (approximately greater than 1.2m), then the light will fade across it. This can be an interesting effect as the light gradients can be quite pleasing, but if objects are to be lit then it may not be practical. In this case horizontal strips would be better, or dividers should be put into the bookcase to allow extra lighting to be installed.

Desks

Many living rooms include a desk where someone can work, often with a computer: perhaps children studying, or a person working from home or merely doing paperwork at the end of the day. The key to lighting a desk is producing a powerful light on the work surface that is not obscured by someone moving around, and it is important that this light does not overpower the rest of the lighting within the room. If the whole room is exposed to the light at the desk, or linked to it, then the environment will be over-lit any time the desk is in use. Since living rooms are commonly used by multiple people at one time, it should be possible to balance the necessary lighting effects in the room to please most occupants. Whatever sort of light is chosen, careful consideration should be given to the heat output. If a light fitting emits a lot of heat towards the desk, then it will make working there very uncomfortable for any extended period of time. Low-heat solutions such as LEDs are excellent options to avoid this.

Desk lamps are the most common type of light for desks. These normally consist of an adjustable arm which allows the light to be directed onto a specific area. They are very good at lighting only the desk, and with the correct shade the light will not spill into other areas of the room. The designs for

desk lamps are endless and choosing one can be difficult. It should give out enough light to work by, although some light sources are not powerful enough to be used for this purpose, so it should be checked what sort of lamp is present within the fitting. If it has an integrated dimmer, then this will allow it also to be used as an ambient light source within the room. Having an adjustable head is very helpful, since the light can be directed. If the lamp is fixed, then it will create a pool of light only in one area. This can be satisfactory on small desks, but larger desks may need more lamps to cover the whole area. Consideration should be given to where the lamp will be connected. There should be a plug socket on the wall near the desk. If there is not, an extension lead may be needed, which can be impractical and unsightly. When producing a lighting plan, it is important to ensure that power sockets are present for any desk or table lamps. If the desk is located away from any walls, such as in a study, then a floor socket may be needed. Floor sockets need to be positioned so that they are accessible, but out of the way so that they do not create a trip hazard. It is best if they can be positioned under the desk itself, so that the cable can be concealed.

Wall lights are sometimes an option if the desk position is fixed. It may be that the desk is built into a cupboard or along a wall, so having wall light spread along this area will illuminate the desk. These could be spotlights, which can direct pools of light onto specific work areas, or they could be more generic wall lights, creating a wash of light across the whole work space. The glare from wall lights can be a problem, so it is best to use a type that relies on indirect lighting. These sorts of fitting wash light downwards (and upwards as well in some cases) onto the work surface, but the body of the fitting prevents the light shining in a person's eyes while they are sitting at the desk.

Downlights are another option. While it can be a little inefficient to light from the ceiling onto the desk, this does allow maximum space on the desk itself. The downlights used should be powerful enough to give a high level of light onto the work surface: anything from 500 to 750 lux is excellent. Multiple downlights should be used and spaced on either side of the desk, angling towards it. If only one downlight is used, then when a person is working at the desk they will create shadows on the surface. Multiple downlights lighting from different directions will reduce the shadows since there will always be a light source from somewhere. Narrow or medium beam widths should be used to focus the light onto the work surface. This will reduce the number of fittings that are needed and prevent the light spilling into the rest of the room. The downlights should be located in front of the chair for the desk so that the user does not block the light.

Open Plan Living Spaces

When creating a design for an open plan living space the critical part is the controls. This particularly affects the living area. While a kitchen is typically always going to require bright lighting, the living room needs as much control over its light levels as possible, so that the correct atmosphere can be created. It is important to have the different areas split up, so that the living area can be lit independently from the rest. It is also desirable to have the lighting adjustable from a position close to the living area, as if the controls for the light levels are located across the room then it is less likely the users will bother to change them. A scene-setting control system provides a good solution to this, especially if there are many circuits within the open plan area. The ability to set different scenes, and control different areas from one location, is both efficient and convenient. It is always best to have a small amount of light in all the rooms, since it can be quite unsettling if the majority of the living space is in darkness while the living room is lit.

AMBIENT LIGHTING

Ambient lighting is very important in a living room. This is what turns the room into a cosy getaway from a long day or a

Photo: The ceiling is uplit from coving with lighting inside. (Lighting design by Leigh Everett. Photo: Mr Resistor)

thunderstorm outside. Soft pools of light that can be dimmed allow the mood to be tailored to whatever is needed. To create good ambient lighting in the living room it is important to layer the light within the space. This can be done by combining the general and task lighting with some ambient lighting. Some fittings have a dual purpose. Table lamps, especially ones that produce both direct and indirect light, can both give good task lighting in their area and also provide excellent ambient light when dimmed. They should be shaded so that there is no glare from the lamp. The light

they emit should be reflected off different surfaces. A standard fabric shade works very well at giving a soft light, and they are available in an almost endless range of different shapes and materials. Normally a table lamp will be able to have different shades fitted onto it, so there are many opportunities for creating an individual style. If the table lamp has a glass or crystal shade then it will give a nice pattern effect, but it will not create a soft light. The same principles apply to floor lamps.

Furniture with built-in lighting, such as the bookcases described earlier, can be an excellent source of ambient light. The light is reflected off the furniture surfaces and throws a soft light back into the room. If the materials of the furniture have warm tones in their finishes, then this will add warmth to the light reflected into the room.

Indirect light from coving or a trough around the ceiling can also introduce a soft light into a living space. While coving or troughs can be applicable in most rooms, the living room is perhaps the best place to use them. The light source is concealed and light washes off the ceiling and back into the room, so there is no glare within the space. If a powerful light source is used, such as high output LED strips or fluorescents, then this can also provide some general light within the room. A similar effect can be created by installing the light fittings on top of full-height cupboards, which both provide a natural platform for mounting the light fittings and conceal them.

Linear lighting can also be built into furniture and architectural details. These details then effectively become light fittings themselves, emitting soft light into the room but without cluttering up the space. Linear lighting can be hidden in skirting, under tables or sofas, and in many other places. If a clean, minimalist style is preferred, hidden linear lighting helps to keep the space clutter-free while simultaneously highlighting the architecture that is so important with this style. It can also be used in other styles of interior,

LED strips built into the furniture on the feature wall and the stairs provide a soft indirect light. (Photo: Marcus Steffen)

though much thought must be given to where the lighting will be fitted to ensure cables are run to the correct points.

CONTROLS

The lighting controls in the living room should provide flexibility over the brightness of each of the lighting circuits. In addition, it is important that the lighting is split up so that there is good control of the different types of lighting within the living area. In a kitchen a bright light is needed, but a living room needs to be able to change completely to a range of different settings. It may be bright when cleaning or working, but then needs to be very low for watching television. For reading in a living room a more relaxed light level is required, with brighter task lighting around the person who is reading.

Individual dimmer switches are very useful within a living room, and having a dimmer switch for every circuit allows the precise tailoring of light within the space. This is much better than a simple on/off control. Individual dimmers will work up to about four lighting circuits. While dimmer switches are available with five or more switches on them, they are large and not very practical. Most people do not bother to adjust each individual circuit to the correct level if there are more than four dimmer switches, and it also makes finding the correct switch quite difficult. Normally they will all just be switched on with a big slap of the hand and left as they are. This is both a waste of electricity and of the time and effort spent creating a good lighting scheme.

Scene-setting systems can be excellent in a living room. Scene-setting allows the pre-setting of the light levels for the different purposes in a living room. At the touch of a button the lighting changes to the most suitable lighting levels. This creates beautiful lighting every time, and prevents the room from appearing over-lit and bland. When choosing a scene-setting system, it is important to select one that can be easily set up and changed. Some systems are restricted to allowing scene-setting only, while others offer scene-setting and individual dimmer control of each circuit. In the living room, there will doubtless need to be some adjustment over time until the settings are ideal. If this requires complicated programming, then people are unlikely to bother and will be left with poor lighting as a result. If there are individual dimmers as well as scene-setting, then it will be possible to temporarily adjust the lighting and find the correct settings, which can then be saved as scenes.

Scene-setting systems are also required if they are going to be integrated with audio-visual systems found in home cinemas and living rooms. An A/V system gives options over the control of the lighting, so it is possible to link into the lights and operate them from a centralized controller or a computer.

CHAPTER 8

ENTERTAINING WITH DRAMA: THE DINING ROOM

The dining room is one of the areas where the majority of people acknowledge the effect that lighting can have. It is even in the name of a type of meal: the candlelit dinner. Meal times are one of those constants in life. They bring friends and family together and form one of the most common meeting points. As well as meal times, dining rooms are often used for paperwork, both for business and for study. It is essential to produce good task lighting over the table, but it is also important to be able to change the atmosphere in the room, to suit the type of meal or the work taking place.

LIGHTING FOR THE TABLE

The focus of any dining area is the table. This is the centre of attention for the room and is generally where any sort of activity takes place. As such, the start of any lighting design for a dining room should focus on how the table will be lit. There are two types of dining table: symmetrical (square or circular) and elongated (rectangular or oval). With a symmetrical shape, it is important to lay out the light fittings around the centre of the table. Most often this is done using one light fitting in the centre, but if the table is large then a circle or square pattern of fittings can also be an option. If the

table is an elongated shape, then the light needs to be spread out along its length, either by placing light fittings along the centre line of the table, or by using a pendant with a long body. If light is placed only over the centre of an elongated table, then there will be an uncomfortably large difference in brightness between the ends and the centre.

Pendants

Pendants over a table provide an excellent focal point for a dining room. Having something decorative hanging above the table helps draw attention to the table itself, and also provides a point of interest for diners at the table. As well as being a beautiful feature, the majority of pendants can change the light emitted from them, in turn changing the feel of the room when lit. This can add another dimension to the mood setting in the dining room. Chandeliers are especially good for this, since their crystals refract the light and create patterns on the surfaces around the room. When choosing a chandelier it is worth examining the crystals and checking their quality, since there are big differences between plain glass, cheap crystals and very high end crystals. This difference is normally found in the pattern of light created when light travels through the crystals, so it is worth while seeing a chandelier lit before purchase.

The placement of pendants can often be quite difficult since the exact position of the table is not normally decided until the room is finished. The cables, however, need to be placed at the first fix stage, before the ceilings are even up, so some careful thinking about how the room will be laid out is very important. Initially, try to obtain an idea of the size and shape of the table, and draw it, to scale, on an architectural plan

OPPOSITE: Feature pendants fill the double height void, while wall lights provide a focal point next to the dining table.

Three chandeliers form a feature over the table, but indirect lighting provides ambient light within the space. (Photo: Mr Resistor)

A chandelier creates a feature over a table, while the downlights wash the walls with light and provide additional general lighting. (Photo: Mr Resistor)

of the dining space, putting it roughly in the centre of the dining room (or the area designated as the dining space in an open plan area). Then add in any other furniture, such as sideboards and dressers. These will affect the placement of the table, since there may not be enough space to walk past the table comfortably or to push chairs out to sit at the table. The table can then be adjusted to a more central position in relation to this furniture. As well as furniture, the pathways around the room need to be considered. In a dedicated dining room with one entrance, the only pathway is generally that round the table. In a room with two or more entrances, there needs to be a clear pathway between the entrances, and this route should be the most direct. In an open plan living space, there needs to be a good flow of pathways between the different areas, and a defined separation in the different spaces, so this can help guide on the placement of the dining table. Once these factors have all been taken into consideration, then the potential positions for the table will be known, allowing the pendants to be placed above it. In some installations it is possible to leave the cable hidden in the ceiling, and at the end, when the final position is decided, a hole can be cut and the cable retrieved. This normally allows a positioning flexibility of approximately 30cm. It is not always possible, though, so should be discussed with the electrician or builder before the first fix (wiring) is done.

A chandelier can be placed at the centre of a symmetrical or elongated table, providing a focal point for the centre of the space. With an elongated table it is possible to have more than one chandelier, though their size and shape need to be appropriate. If the chandelier is too wide, then the light will overlap the edge of the table, and this can be quite uncomfortable for the guests sitting under it. It may also draw attention away from the table, and its shape and impact in the room will be lost. Having two or three smaller chandeliers gives a good spread of light and decoration, while still remaining in proportion to the table. Chandeliers are also available in almost any shape, so a long rectangular or curved chandelier could be used above an elongated table to emphasize the design.

The mounting height of a chandelier or pendant over a dining room table can vary dramatically. It is best to look at the purpose of these lights first before determining at what height they should be mounted. If they are merely intended to create a decorative effect above the table, and the task lighting for the table will be produced by a different light source, then the mounting height is purely aesthetic, and should be determined by the style and size of the light fitting in proportion to the table and the rest of the room. If they are providing the task lighting for the table, then they must be mounted at a height to produce a sufficient light level on the table. The table is also the focus of the space, so some contrast is desired between it and the surrounding areas, so that it stands out and becomes the object of attention. If the pendant has a controlled light output, such as a shade directing the light downwards, then as well as mounting it at a height to provide good light, it should be installed in the best position so that the light falls only on the table rather than lighting the whole area. A good result may be obtained with the pendant hung low over a table, just washing onto the table surface, and not producing any glare for the surrounding diners. Once all of these factors have been determined and checked, it is worth considering the sight lines in the room. If a pendant or chandelier is hung low over a table, it may block a view out of a window, ruining one of the best features of the room. If so, perhaps a different style of light would be better, or perhaps the view is less important than the interior design of the table and pendants together. Glass or chrome pendants are less intrusive, so may offer a compromise in the design to maintain some of the view.

Downlights

Downlights are another option to place above a table. They provide a high level of light and can be distributed above the table, meaning they can be used to illuminate any shape of table efficiently. It is important to use the correct beam angles on the downlights to ensure that the light contacts the table and does not spill too far over the edge. It is also worth considering having a narrow beam spotlight over the centre of the table, to highlight a bunch of flowers or a centrepiece, giving a focal point. If using downlights, it is best to make sure that they have anti-glare features, since it is essential to have the option of soft light in the dining room. They should also be dimmable, allowing the tailoring of the atmosphere of the room depending on the type of experience wanted while dining or working. If there is a choice, low-voltage halogen is ideal, since the warmer light at low level and the cooler white at full brightness will cater for almost all settings. If this is not possible, then using a warm-coloured lamp, around 2700K, will give the best results.

Downlights also provide a good solution if it is not pos-

An extension used as a dining area with decorative wall lights and a suspended wire system for lighting the table. (Photo: Mr Resistor)

sible to determine the final position of the table, or if it may be changed over time. Sometimes extendable tables do not have the centre in the same place once they are extended, so a pendant or chandelier will not work. With downlights there could be two separate circuits to light the table, one for when it is compressed, the other for when it is extended. Adjustable downlights should be used because this allows the table to be positioned off-centre, and the light can be directed to fall onto the table. It is important to ensure that the downlights are not angled too far. Most downlights have a maximum tilt of 30°, but some, such as scoop fittings can tilt much further. This is not a good idea when lighting onto a table though,

since the person sitting opposite an over-tilted downlight will see the lamp shining directly towards them, producing a large amount of glare and making it very unpleasant to look straight ahead.

Track Lighting

Track lighting is a good solution when working with a flexible space. The track can be mounted along the centre line of the table, and spotlights added along its length to light the table. This gives a highly adjustable lighting solution, since it is very easy to reposition the spotlights at any time, and they can be moved along the track as required. Track lighting is an excellent solution for tables that are moved frequently or can change drastically in shape and size. Some tables are modular, and so may be formed into squares or long rectangles. The track lighting can be repositioned at any time to focus onto the table surface, allowing excellent task lighting. The range of track spotlights is almost endless, with types available to suit particular needs. Beam widths can be easily chosen and changed, and the type of light can be varied. If a multi-circuit track is used, then different groupings of fittings can be used to produce different lighting layouts, making the transition even easier. It is also very easy to upgrade to different light sources as they become available, without extensive rewiring. Track lighting does have the disadvantage of being highly visible, so it is not always suitable in certain designs, such as those incorporating a very traditional sense of style. Sometimes it is good to have a contrast with the design of the room, such as incorporating a very industrial style of fitting. Since track lighting is generally used within the commercial sector, there is a wide range of styles available, from sleek, minimalist designs to futuristic LED fittings. It is even possible to hang pendants from a track system, allowing for the addition of features over the table.

As with downlights, it is important to incorporate anti-glare features into track-mounted spotlights. Since they can be tilted to an almost horizontal direction, there is a high risk of glare, and this should be borne in mind when designing the track layout. It is also important to think about the height of the ceiling. If the ceiling is low, then track fittings must not be mounted where they can be walked into, which can be dangerous. At least 25cm should be allowed for the drop in the ceiling height for track, so generally the ceiling needs to be at least 2.4m high to accommodate track lighting.

Wire Systems

Wire lighting systems are another alternative for lighting over a table. They are especially suitable for elongated tables, where multiple spots are needed in a line. While not as flexible as track lighting, since fittings cannot generally be moved once installed, wire systems do provide a degree of flexibility in the set up. Since power is normally drawn from one of the ends, the wires will have some leeway in positioning, and this can be done at the end of a project, allowing the table to

be positioned correctly. Wire systems can have a variety of fittings attached to them, depending on the manufacturer, since there is no standardized wire system. It is an excellent solution where light fittings cannot be installed in the ceiling above the table, such as in a vaulted ceiling or a glass skylight. It enables light to be placed in the correct place, but without the construction problems.

Wall and Floor Lights

Specialist wall and floor lights are available which serve the purpose of lighting a table. The most famous of these is the Arco lamp, designed by Achille and Pier Giacomo Castiglioni for Flos; it has a shaded lamp mounted on a large curved arm, which is cantilevered over the table by a large marble base. This fitting has been copied numerous times and various different styles of this type of fitting are available, but it is hard to better the original. There are number of wall lights that use a cantilevered arm with a lamp on the end to position the light over the table while avoiding being a nuisance to the diners. It is important to know the distance the table will be from the wall, because these lights have a maximum extension.

GENERAL LIGHTING

Once the lighting for the table has been selected, it is necessary to arrange the rest of the lighting in the room. This should complement the lighting over the table without detracting from it, so it is worth considering discreet fittings rather than large, intrusive ones. In a dining room, soft ambient light is also wanted, to allow the creation of an inviting, comfortable atmosphere.

Downlights provide a practical general light in the dining area, but it should be remembered that these are not particularly good at creating a soft ambience. It is best to use the downlights as accent lights, highlighting features in the room, such as artwork and furniture, rather than covering the whole space with them. This allows the focus to be drawn to these feature pieces. If using downlights, try not to position them directly above a seat, since the light effect can be harsh on the person sitting there. It is not very complimentary to have dramatic shadows cast across someone's face, not to mention potential problems with heat.

A skylight fitted with small star lights and downlights to provide additional lighting and reduce shadows within the cavity. (Photo: Mr Resistor)

Uplighting and indirect lighting offer a fantastic way to complement the lighting over the table. With wall lights or table lamps it is possible to wash light across the ceiling of a room, and provide both a good ambience when dimmed, and a practical light when at full power. Table lamps can work very well on a sideboard in the dining room, especially when used in pairs. They can also provide a beautiful decorative feature by producing overlapping patterns of light on the wall. It is best to use fittings with shades, rather than exposed lamps, since the glare needs to be reduced. This ensures the light is emitted up and down, rather than glaring in a diner's eyes on the other side of the room. Another option is a coffer around the surround of the room, providing a wash of light onto the ceiling and indirect light reflected into the space. This can produce a feeling of height within a room, which can be useful in small spaces. If a full coffer is not suitable, due to design or construction issues, then uplighting from built-in furniture is also a good option. For example, in traditional Victorian and Georgian houses, the dining room is generally centred around a fireplace, with a tall cupboard on either side. Uplighting from the top of each of these cupboards can provide a good source of indirect lighting, which can be complemented with a sideboard and two table lamps on the opposite side of the room.

CONTROLS

The dining room normally has simple controls. Dimmers are essential for setting the mood, but there are normally not many circuits to control. Having dimmer switches allows the fine tuning of the light to exactly the right levels, and can make for a much more comfortable atmosphere while eating. Scene-setting can also be beneficial, and can ensure that the light levels are always appropriate to the use of the room. After cooking a big meal, it can be a little much to come in and start adjusting the light settings, when everyone is hungry and just wants to eat. A scene-setting system allows the lighting to be changed at the touch of a button, with the most commonly used levels pre-programmed into the system. If a scene-setting system is being used, then it must be one that allows the client to tailor the light levels. More sophisticated lighting control systems require a specialist to come in and do the set up. While this is fine initially, if they have to come back regularly because the owner wants to have the light levels adjusted all the time then this will be both impractical and very costly. Most good systems allow the adjustment of light levels by the owner rather than requiring a programmer to attend site. Some of the more basic systems are actually designed to be set up by the owner, and these may be more suitable for a dining room. Having accessible dimmers on the control unit, as well as the scene buttons, will make it much easier to tailor the lighting for those special events, such as Christmas or a big dinner party.

CHAPTER 9

THE RETREAT FROM THE WORLD: THE BEDROOM

Good bedroom lighting can be difficult to achieve. There needs to be a balance between powerful, practical light and relaxed soft light. The key is to blend both direct task lighting and soft ambient light and then balance this using dimmer switches or scene-setting controls.

It is essential to know the layout of the bedroom before starting the lighting design. There is normally a large amount of furniture in a bedroom, and this may restrict the placement of wall lights and table lamps, which are key to achieving the soft, ambient light needed for creating a relaxed atmosphere. If furniture is built-in, it can provide excellent positions to install built-in indirect lighting, and can also be fitted with interior cupboard lighting, which helps reduce the requirement for task lighting externally located from the cupboards.

General lighting does not need to be as powerful as in a kitchen, since fewer intensive tasks are carried out in the bedroom. Normally good task lighting is provided in the few spaces where it is needed. Ambient light is essential in a bedroom. To create a feeling of relaxation and calm both before sleeping and when waking up it is important to provide a gentle transition between light and darkness. Light fittings with little to no glare should be used, softening even the general light. With built-in furniture it is quite simple to provide uplighting from fluorescents or LEDs which will be dimmable.

OPPOSITE: Wall lights provide general lighting while the table lamps provide task light for the bed.

A warm colour should be used, though it is possible to do both a warm colour and a cool colour to provide a simulation of daylight.

TASK LIGHTING

Bedside Lighting

For bedside lighting, knowing the bed position is essential. There are normally one or two options, but many people leave the decision until much later. However, it is worth making the decision early on so that the lighting can be tailored around the bed position. Some flexibility can be built into the lighting layout if it really cannot be fixed early. Generally it is not a good idea to mount lights directly above the bed. When lying in bed, people tend to look straight up at the ceiling, and it would be very uncomfortable to look directly at a spotlight located above the head of the bed. This is especially a problem in a bedroom, where the light level is normally lower than in other rooms. The same can be said about hanging pendants over the bed.

When trying to provide light around the bed itself, it is important to consider what it will be needed for. Reading in bed is common, and so lighting should be provided around the head of the bed. This can be done by table lamps positioned on bedside tables, wall lights mounted to the left and right of the bed, or even small built-in LED reading lights. Caution should be taken with wall lights, since they need to be positioned in exactly the right location relative to the bed. This is easy to do in a symmetrical room, but in an asymmetrical room it may be difficult to get the position right. Careful

Two bedside lights and a crystal pendant provide dramatic lighting as well as general bedroom illumination. (Design by Leigh Everett. Photo: Mr Resistor)

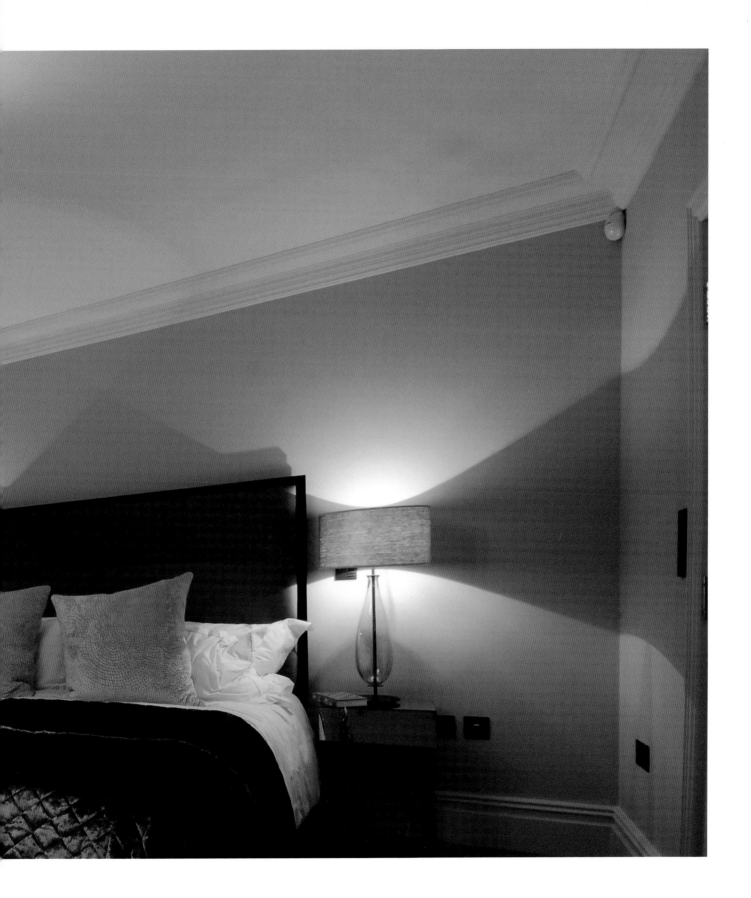

planning, perhaps including elevation drawings or 3D representations, is needed before the wiring is installed.

Table lamps are an easy option, providing excellent light and features within the room. It is strongly recommended that they are plugged into a lighting socket, sometimes known as a 5A or 2A socket. These differ from a standard 13A socket in having round prongs. There can be multiple sockets installed on a lighting circuit, and they can all be controlled from a central dimmer switch. This gives the ability both to turn on and off all the table and floor lamps together, or to dim them to a particular brightness. This is very convenient, especially if there are many table lamps within the room. Most table and floor lamps come supplied with 13A plugs, but is a very simple task to change them to 5A or 2A plugs. The 5A plug is bigger than a 2A plug, so care should be taken to purchase the correct plug to match the socket installed in the wall. Care

should also be taken when selecting table lamps. Some have transformers or in-built dimmers. These cannot be centrally dimmed, and could potentially be damaged if used in this way. The supplier should be able to tell you if a lamp has an in-built dimmer or transformer.

There is a range of small LED reading lights that can either be fixed to the wall as wall lights or built into the bed itself. These normally provide a focused beam of light on an adjustable head, and this can be used to provide good light for reading, while not illuminating the surrounding area. While these are functional task lights, they will not add to the lighting of the room. If it is planned to build the lighting into the bed itself, it is worth building in a switch as well. Having individually switched lights inside a bed enables better control, and if all the necessary transformers or drivers are also built into the bed, it will be possible to place a power lead with

Bedside table lamps provide soft pools of light, while a fluorescent strip in the shadow gap of the ceiling washes the curtains with light. (Photo: Mr Resistor)

Two wall lights used as bedside lights that also create a decorative light pattern. (Photo: Mr Resistor)

a 13A plug onto it as well. This means that the bed can be removed without rewiring, and can even be moved to a new position or even a new house without losing the lighting that has been designed for it.

If there is built-in furniture surrounding the bed, then it may be possible to build the lighting into this furniture, and then almost anything is possible, from alcove lighting to spotlights and wall lights. Time should be taken to design this furniture early on, so that the lighting can be incorporated into it. It is wise to run some power to this furniture, even if it the final choice is not decided on early on. This power supply can then be connected to any lighting in the furniture, and extra wiring can be added as it is installed.

Wardrobe and Cupboard Lighting

One of the main purposes of a bedroom, along with providing somewhere to rest, is as a place for changing clothes. Whether it is getting ready for work in the morning, preparing for an evening out or changing into nightwear at the end of the day, there needs to be good lighting for both changing and also choosing the right clothes. It is essential to provide task lighting onto or inside the wardrobes present inside a bedroom.

If free-standing or pre-made furniture is being used in the room, then it may not be possible to build this lighting into the furniture. In this case, providing downlights in the ceiling gives the best light. These can be angled into the wardrobe, giving good light into the interior of the wardrobe so that clothing can be seen. It is important to position these lights well so that when someone opens the wardrobe, they do not block the light. Installing these lights quite close, between 300 and 600mm away from the face of the wardrobe, reduced this problem of shadowing. It might also be necessary to allow two spotlights for a wardrobe, one positioned on either side. This way there can be a crossover of light into the wardrobe, and this further reduces the risk of shadows.

If the furniture is built into the building, or will be permanently fixed in place, then lighting can be built into the furniture, providing both an interesting feature and practical task lighting. It is important to liaise with both the furniture-maker and the electrician when designing built-in lighting. The furniture-maker will need to allow for cables to be installed, as well as access points and space for transformers, and the instal-

lation space for the lighting. The electrician will be able to advise on what is possible, and what sort of space is required for the components of the lighting, as well as being able to ensure that when it is finished it complies with all the regulations and is safe for use.

The aim of built-in lighting inside wardrobes is to provide light onto the items inside. Before approaching the lighting design, it is necessary to know the layout of any hanging rails, shelves and drawers. It is best to draw out each wardrobe in elevation with these details in place, and then start to think about where the lighting may be positioned. The most common place to install lighting is across the top of the cupboard. This is unobtrusive and easy to install, and gives a wash of light inside. Unfortunately, this is not normally adequate for the purpose of providing light through the whole cupboard. The light from the top will be blocked by hanging clothes or shelves, and will provide little or no illumination at the bottom

Wardrobes highlighted by downlights, providing both a feature and task lighting. (Photo: Mr Resistor)

of the cupboard, where it is normally the darkest. A better solution is to provide light down either side of the cupboard, lighting horizontally onto any shelves or hanging items. This gives a more even light throughout the wardrobe, and provides lots of light at the base, where there is normally a messy pile of shoes and miscellaneous items. The key to doing this well lies in concealing it correctly. The lighting can either be recessed into the side of the furniture, or a lip must be provided on either side to conceal it. LED strips are normally the most convenient item to use for this purpose. They have a reduced heat output, and are generally very small, meaning they can be built in very easily.

Drawers can be more difficult to provide light for, since positioning the light can be quite difficult. It is possible to have a light built inside the drawer which is then turned on with a switch or sensor when it is opened. Another alternative is to mount a light in the top of the drawer unit, with an overhang. The light sits in front of the face of the drawers, and when one is opened, the light shines down onto its contents.

If the furniture is to be left open, without doors, then it is best to control this lighting with a switch inside the room. This can also provide illumination into the room as well, as an indirect light source. It is not ideal, though, especially if the wardrobes are not likely to be kept in an immaculate state. Generally open cupboards are found only in dedicated dressing-rooms or walk-in wardrobes. If the cupboards are fitted with doors, then the lights will have to be controlled using a switch or sensor that works when the doors are opened. If hinged doors are being used, then a door switch is a practical option. Some door switches require the weight of the door to be against them. If light doors are used, then they may not turn the switch off, meaning the light stays on all the time. It is important to test the door switch before installation, since it will be expensive to replace later on, with considerable work needed to replace sections of the furniture. Sensors that work by motion detection can also be used. It is important to select the right sensor and angle it in the right direction so that it activates when the door is opened. If sliding doors are chosen, then door switches become very difficult to use. In this case built-in sensors are the best solution. Most sensors have a transformer or control pack, so consideration should be given as to where this can be located. Normally there is a void at the top or bottom of a cupboard, and this can be a good location, with access via a removable panel or trim in case of electrical failure.

GENERAL LIGHTING

Once all the areas discussed above have been lit, there remains the task of providing general light within the bedroom. This does not need to be particularly powerful, since bedrooms do not need high light levels. As long as there is task lighting, then the general lighting is of secondary importance. Sometimes it will not be necessary to provide general lighting if table lamps are used around the room for ambience, since at full power these can to provide a large amount of light. If extra lighting is required, then it is vital that the glare from these additional lights should be reduced, to make the room feel more comfortable.

Downlights are a good option to place pools of light around a room where they are needed to boost the light levels, without flooding the space and creating a bland wash of light. Baffles should be used in the fittings to reduce the glare from them, and generally they should not be positioned above the bed if it can be avoided. The bed is one of the few areas in the house where a person looks directly up. If there is a downlight above them shining directly downwards then there will be a large amount of glare, and this could make the bed quite uncomfortable. If there are really no other options, then it is a good idea to use adjustable downlights with baffles, and place them on either side, using one side to angle across to the opposite side of the bed and vice versa. This way the light is at least at an angle, so that the user has some protection from the glare. Honeycomb baffles are best for this sort of use, since even when the light fitting is tilted slightly they give maximum protection from glare.

Wall lights can be used to great effect in a bedroom to give a good indirect light. Wall-mounted uplights are especially good for washing ceilings with light and creating a general light. If these are dimmable as well, then they can create a soft light within the room which is very important. When planning the room, it is best to work out where the furniture will be before committing to positioning the wall lights. If most of the walls will be covered in wardrobes or cupboards, then wall lights will either need to be removed or repositioned, and so it is best to start this planning early on. A cupboard might be placed on one side of a wall, but if the wall light has been centred on this wall without taking the cupboard into account, then it will appear to be too close to it in the finished room. The wall light should be centred on the wall space where it is mounted. If the furniture is not as high as the wall light itself, and the difference in height is adequate, then

Light reflected off a mirror table creates a dramatic effect in a bedroom. (Photo: Mr Resistor)

this may not matter. This is often the case with high-ceilinged rooms, where the furniture may only reach to 2.3m, but the wall lights are mounted at 2.7m.

There should always be sufficient distance between the wall light and the ceiling. If it is too close, then a bright spot of light will appear on the ceiling, rather than a wash across the whole space. This spacing depends on the light fitting chosen, and can only be determined through trial and error. Asking the manufacturer or an expert might give some guidance. It is also worth checking with the electrician if the cable can be left in the wall, with some excess, so that once the correct height is determined, a small hole can be drilled through to retrieve it. This is not always possible, but it can provide some

flexibility both in choosing a fitting and mounting it at the right height.

Wall lights cannot always be used, generally due to the quantity of furniture placed in a bedroom and the resulting lack of suitable fixing surfaces. In this case it is worth considering a linear wash of light, either washing up onto the ceiling or down the walls. If washing up into the ceiling, then there will normally need to be two levels, with the lower around the sides to allow for a trough to mount the lighting in. As an alternative, if there are many high cupboards within the room, strips can be placed on top of them. Sometimes it is possible to create a recess in the top of the wall to conceal the lighting inside. This has the advantage of not having to create

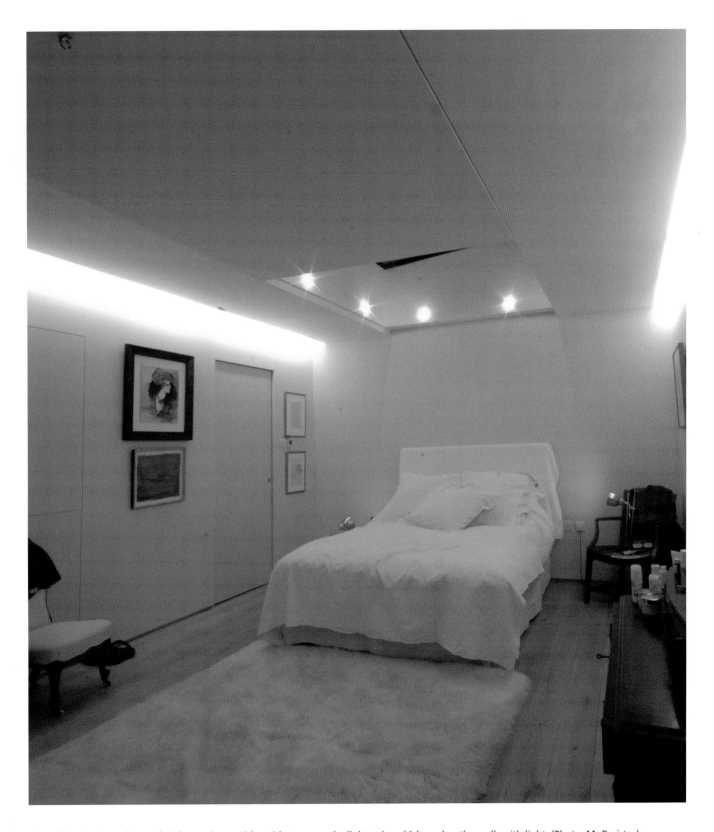

The ceiling has been lowered with a cavity on either side to conceal a light strip, which washes the walls with light. (Photo: Mr Resistor)

two different levels of ceiling, but does make the construction of the wall more complex. This is one of the most discreet solutions, though, since the architectural lines of the room are unchanged.

As an alternative to washing the ceiling, the walls could be washed. Generally a shadow gap is created into which the linear lighting is mounted. If there is a lot of furniture in the room, then this is not always the best idea, but it is useful to wash down a feature wall. Another fantastic use for this method is to wash light down curtains and blinds, highlighting them at night. If shutters or Venetian blinds are to be used, then this can produce a very interesting pattern of light and shadow as each of the slats shields a portion of the one below.

No matter which method is used, it is important to make sure that the lighting is shielded from direct view. This can be done with a small pelmet along the edge, with the lighting concealed behind it. The height of this edge is very important. If it is too tall, then it will block too much light, but if it is too low the fittings will be visible and the effect will be ruined. In most cases it is best to have it slightly taller than the fittings being used. The edge should be finished in a clean, straight line. If it is rough or jagged, then this will be seen in the light washing across the ceiling. The positioning of the linear strip of lighting is important too. If it is too close to this lip, then the light will be cut off prematurely, creating a border of light around the room with a sharp cut-off. Placing the light further back allows the light to spread across more of the ceiling, giving a more even wash. The same can be said for lights concealed in a shadow gap, washing down walls.

CONTROLS

The bedroom is the area which needs the most control over the light within it. Being able to adjust the light levels from a bright setting to something that can be used in the middle of the night is essential. Dimmer switches are the simplest control method, and provide a good option for a bedroom due to the fine control they give over the light levels within the room. When positioning the switches in the bedroom, the ideal is to have one set by the doorway, and two others, one on either side of the bed. Since only one of these can be a dimmer set, it is best to position this on one side of the bed. Most adjustments are made when getting into or out of bed, so it is helpful to have the switch here, rather than over by the door. Normally all that needs to take place by the door is switching on and off.

It may be worth investigating more sophisticated systems that allow multiple dimming points. These systems have only one dimmer switch, but have multiple buttons linked back to it. Wireless switches are common. They use a radio signal to transmit a command back to a centralized dimmer, telling

CHILDREN'S BEDROOMS

Children's bedrooms are an exception to most of the rules for bedroom lighting, as they tend to be used in an entirely different way than adults' bedrooms. A child's bedroom is the one space where they have control of what takes place there. They use it for playing with friends, studying and relaxing away from the family. Whereas an adult's bedroom is only used early in the morning and late at night, a child's bedroom may be used all through the day, and for many different purposes. As such, the lighting needs to be much more flexible. Added to these extra requirements, there is the factor that as children grow and develop, so their tastes and interests change too. The décor and furniture needs to adapt as they grow, and the layout may be altered every year. Due to this changing environment, it is worth producing a generic general lighting layout in the room to cater for all eventualities. Downlights spread evenly across the room or an uplit ceiling with the fittings hidden in a trough or coving will allow the lighting to work in almost any situation. Anti-glare fittings will reduce glare in most options for the bed position. 5A sockets scattered around the room also provide flexibility in placing table and floor lamps, both for task lighting and for ambience. If possible, it is nice to work in a fun feature for a child's bedroom. This can be something extravagant, such as a star ceiling created with fibre optics, or something simple like a colour-changing table lamp. This feature can add some individuality to a room, and provides the child with something to show off to their friends.

Wall lights that give an indirect light are excellent in a bedroom due to the reduced glare. (Photo: Mr Resistor)

it to dim up or down. Multiple switches can be programmed to the same dimmer, and will all be able to vary the light or turn it on and off. This enables dimming from both sides of the bed and the entrance, increasing flexibility and reducing installation costs, since there is less wiring. Wireless switches can even be incorporated into bed heads, making them more accessible than conventional switches on the wall.

If a wireless system is not used, then the positioning of the switches next to the bed is crucial. If they are too close, they may be covered up by the headboard, and if too far away, they may be difficult to reach. Thus it is important to decide on the size of the bed and the headboard, and the bed's position in the room so that the switch positions can be determined. As well as a layout plan, it may be worth doing an elevation drawing of the wall with the bed on it to look at the proportions before finalizing the switch positions. Once the cables are in place, they will need to be ripped out and

moved if the switch position changes, so it is important to get it right first time.

Scene-setting is also very useful within a bedroom, although it is unlikely that there will be much variation. The most common settings include a general fully lit scene, a relaxed scene and a night-time scene. The relaxed scene will have the majority of circuits dimmed down, with perhaps the bedside lights and ambient lighting turned up a little brighter than the general lighting. The night-time setting is for use after going to sleep. It brings on one circuit at a very low level, allowing the user, who will have good night vision at this point, to get up and be able to manoeuvre around the room without bumping into furniture. This can be helpful for when one partner needs to get up earlier than the other, so that they can go to the bathroom and get ready without waking the other one up. Of course, there may be more settings, but these are the most common.

CHAPTER 10

LIGHTING CONTROLS

All light fittings need to be controlled, and the variety of different control systems available is bewildering. From basic on/off switches to a computer-controlled lighting system for a whole house, the choice can be vast and can affect a project in dramatic ways. The key to designing a good control system for the lighting is to make it simple and accessible. A few people want to have a system where they can adjust everything, from the fade time to what time of day the lights can come on and off, but most simply want to be able to turn the lights on when they enter a room, and set the light levels to suit its current purpose. This is not to say that automated systems are not practical, but they must be set up correctly so that anyone in the property has intuitive control over the lighting. If a guest cannot use an unfamiliar light switch, then the lighting controls are not fulfilling their purpose. All lighting controls are there to enable control over the light in the room.

When producing a lighting design, it is always the lighting that is finished first, never the control system. The lighting must be correct, and the circuits of how it will be controlled should be decided on from an aesthetic point of view. There will be lighting circuits that need to be controlled separately since they have

different purposes in a room. For example, downlights providing general light in a room need to be controlled separately from wall lights that create a soft ambient light. If they were controlled together, then the downlights would overpower the effect of the wall lights, and render them pointless. If the controls are decided on before the lighting is finalized, then the type of lighting and the breakdown of the circuits will be forced to conform to a pre-set number. This may result in too much money being spent on a control system with an over-

OPPOSITE: Recessed uplights highlight the underside of the floating staircase.

RIGHT: A Lutron Grafik Eye provides scene-setting and individual dimming control. (Photo: Mr Resistor)

sized capacity, or circuits may need to be linked, hampering the creation of an effective lighting system, and defeating the purpose of the lighting controls.

One feature that is common in almost all switches is the need for a back box to be fitted into the wall. This allows the switch to be recessed into the wall cavity so that it does not protrude from the wall. There are standard sizes and depths for back boxes, but these vary between countries, so if a system is being purchased from abroad it is best to check what sort of back box is needed. Different styles of switches need different depths. Most back boxes are 35mm deep, but some need to be deeper, especially if there are many switches on the plate, since extra space is needed for cables. The required depth of the back boxes should be checked with the manufacturer or supplier, and discussed with the electrician and builder to ensure that it is possible in all locations. Some areas cannot have switches because there is inadequate depth for the back boxes within the wall. A good example of this is walls with pocket doors concealed within them. The structural build-up around the door will reduce the cavity into which the back box can be placed.

CONVENTIONAL SWITCHING

On/Off Switches

The most basic control for lighting is a switch that turns a

A two-gang antique bronze toggle switch, sometimes called a dolly switch. (Photo: Mr Resistor)

circuit on and off. This provides very basic control over what lighting is on within a space, and can be found in almost every home. There are many different styles of switch, but all control the lighting circuit in the same way. Multiple switches can be used to control the same lighting circuit, which is important when there is more than one entrance into a room. These need a particular wiring layout, but this has been the same for a long time and all electricians are trained in this work.

Three types of switch are used for operating lighting. One-way switches are the most basic type. The live wire is connected through the switch, going in one side and out the other. When the switch is opened or closed, the flow of the current to the light circuit is controlled, turning it on or off. Unfortunately, this break in the circuit means that if two of these switches are wired on the same circuit, and one of them is open, the other will not function.

Two-way switches work in the same way as one-way switches, but have two outputs rather than one. This allows two wires to be connected from a switch to another two-way switch and its corresponding outputs. For example, if the first switch is in the 1 position, and the second switch is in the 2 position, then there is no electrical connection and the lights will be off. If the first switch is then changed to the 2 position, it will create a connection with the second switch and the current will flow, switching on the circuit.

When three or more switches are required, then intermediate switches are used. In a circuit with three switches, there will be a two-way switch at either end, and an intermediate

A three-gang satin nickel trimless rocker switch. (Photo: Mr Resistor)

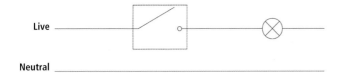

One-way wiring using a one-way switch. (Diagram: Marcus Steffen)

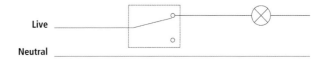

One-way wiring using a two-way switch. (Diagram: Marcus Steffen)

Two-way wiring. (Diagram: Marcus Steffen)

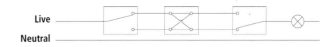

Three-way wiring using two two-way switches and an intermediate switch. (Diagram: Marcus Steffen)

switch in the middle. This switch breaks the two wires running between the two-way switches and allows them to be crossed over to make a connection. An intermediate switch has four connections: two inputs and two outputs. When the intermediate switch is in its first switch position, input one will be connected to output one and input two connected to output two. In its second switch position, input one will be connected to output two, and input two connected to output one. This allows all three switches to work together, and each one will be able to turn the lights on and off. If more switches are needed, then extra intermediates are wired into the circuit.

It is not essential to know how switches are wired up and how they function, but it is important to know what needs to be purchased for a project when specifying the types of switch to be used. One-way switches are rarely used since two-way switches can be used instead, and there is barely any difference in cost. This simplifies the purchasing of all the switches for a property. If three or more switches are needed for a circuit, then one of them must be an intermediate switch. Some switch manufacturers make a modular system of switches, sometimes called grid switches. Each switch is fixed to the switch plate separately, so it is easier to combine two-way and intermediate switches on the same plate. Other manufacturers use moulded switches, so they are all part of the same module. These will all be of one type, normally two-way, so if an intermediate is needed, then it will have to be a separate switch on the wall. It is useful to know which type of switch is being used when doing the lighting design so that the correct wall boxes can be allowed in the wall.

Wireless Switching

Wireless switching is a relatively new development within the lighting industry, but the technology has been around for a long time. It has long been used for remote locking for cars, as well as the remote operation of blinds and shutters. For wireless lighting there are generally two components: a transmitter and a receiver. The receiver is wired into the lighting circuit before the light fittings, and controls the process of switching or dimming. The transmitter is a switch, normally battery-powered, that sends a signal to the receiver. When the receiver picks up this signal, it will respond with whatever function it has been programmed to do, either turning the light on or off or dimming it up or down.

Using wireless lighting reduces the amount and complexity of wiring in a property. For example, in a hallway with a lighting circuit there may be three switches. These would normally be wired in the two-way plus intermediate configuration detailed above, requiring a large number of cables to be run around the room. Using wireless switching, the single receiver needs to be wired into the lighting circuit, and then the three wireless switches will be placed in the appropriate positions. These all communicate back to the receiver, meaning no cables need to be run to them. This can make installation very quick and reduces the cost of labour on site.

Receivers are available to control almost any dimming type, and the switches are available in a range of different styles and finishes. It is worth noting that wireless does not mean that it will work with a home computer network. These operate on

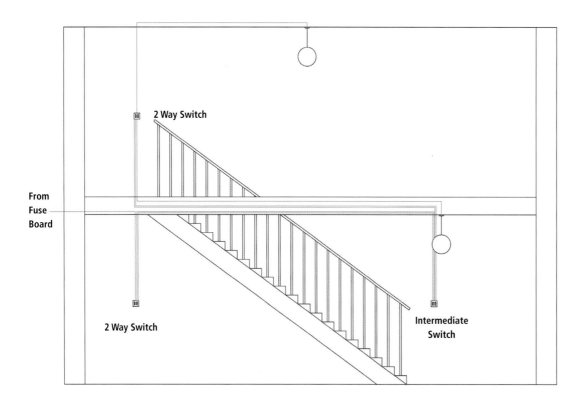

2 Way Switch

From Fuse Board

2 Way Switch

Intermediate Switch

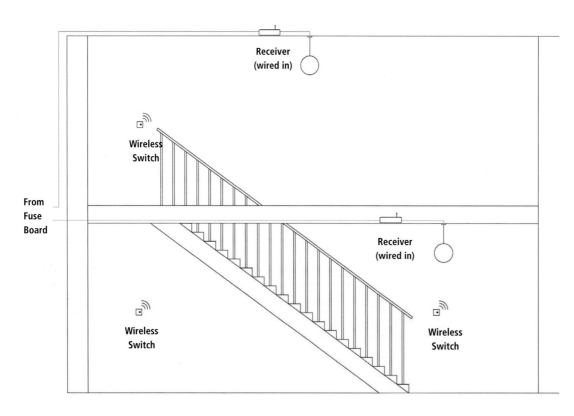

Receiver (wired in)

Wireless Switch

From Fuse Board

Receiver (wired in)

Wireless Switch

Wireless Switch

An example of wireless switching in a room, showing how the installation of two-way wiring cable is unnecessary. (Diagram: Marcus Steffen)

different frequencies and with different programming types, and are not compatible unless the wireless controls manufacturer produces some sort of interface.

Passive Infra-red Sensors

Passive infra-red (PIR) sensors are detectors that measure changes in temperature within a certain area. They can detect the movement of a person since all people emit a certain amount of infra-red heat, sometimes called body heat. This is 'seen' by the sensor, which can differentiate between the person and any background emissions, and switches on an electrical circuit. PIR sensors are most commonly used for external security lighting, and internally on burglar alarms, but they can be used for other purposes as well. One good

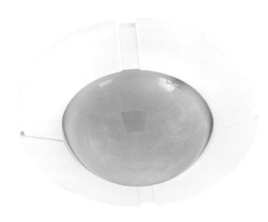

A recessed PIR sensor, which can detect motion within the room, activating the lights. (Photo: Mr Resistor)

use is to have a sensor switching lights on in an infrequently used area, such as a utility room or pantry. The lights will automatically switch on, and once the room is vacated they will switch off after a certain amount of time. Sensors are also commonly used within wardrobes with doors. When a door is opened, the sensor activates the internal lights and illuminates the wardrobe, but when the door is closed the lights switch off.

Sensors can also be used to control dramatic effect lighting within a space. For example, in a hallway there may be some sort of effect lighting, such as uplights framing the doorways.

As soon as a person walks into this space, a sensor can be used to switch these uplights on, highlighting the doorways in stark contrast to the surrounding walls. If needed, other lighting can then be turned on. Sensors can also be used to control low-level walkway and stair lighting, and even lighting in the bathroom for late-night visits. This saves having to find the correct switch, and if the lighting is adequate then other lighting will not need to be turned on, reducing energy consumption.

Sensors are wired in instead of switches. If a switch is connected, then it will do one of two things. Either the switch will disable the sensor, ensuring that the lighting remains off when it should come on, or it will turn the lights permanently on, overriding the sensor, even if there is no one within the space where the sensor is located.

Timers

Timers are simple controls that turn lighting circuits on and off at certain times of the day. There are different types of timer switches available. Some control the lighting at predetermined times over a 24-hour period, while others operate over a week, allowing variations depending on the day. External timer sensors can be set to turn on at dusk and turn off again at dawn, or after a certain period of time. There are also astronomical time clocks that can be programmed with a world location and a date, and operate to the seasonal light changes. These are common in sophisticated, whole-house lighting control systems.

Timers are excellent for simple security measures and also for operating outdoor lighting. They ensure lighting is not left on when there is too much daylight, and turn it off when it is not needed.

DIMMING CONTROL

Dimmer switches are a key component in a lighting system. The ability to set the level of light output from each of the light circuits in the room allows the entire space to be changed, from a bright, functional space to a warm, inviting area to curl up and watch a movie or read a book. Control of the light levels within a room is essential to a lighting design, and should only be omitted within spaces that have only one purpose, such as a utility room or cupboard. Even here, it may be worth having some form of dimmer control linked to the daylight level within the space to save energy.

Dimming control allows the user to adjust the ambience of a room, but it also saves energy and prolongs the life of the lamps. This energy saving depends on the lamp type, but in almost all cases it is significant. The lamp life is also extended with most lamps. In the case of incandescent lamps, the lamp life can be doubled or tripled by dimming. Some dimmers use a slow fade on and fade off. This gradually applies the electric current, rather than turning it on to full power straight away. This is pleasant for the user, as the light slowly turns on or off over a few seconds, but also extends lamp life since they do not have to tolerate sudden large changes of current.

The golden rule for dimmers is that there can only ever be one. A dimmer switch works by either switching the electrical current on and off very rapidly (conventional dimmers) or by sending some form of dimming signal (0–10V, DALI, etc.). If there is more than one dimmer, it will cause a conflict on the electrical circuit and the light fitting will try to achieve two different brightness levels at once. It may appear that some control systems have multiple dimmer switches, but this is not the case. These systems use the switch buttons to send a signal back to a centralized dimmer that controls the lighting. By this method it is possible to have more than one control switch, but there will always be only one dimmer.

A clear perspex rotary dimmer switch. (Photo: Mr Resistor)

A Wise Controls Fusion dimmer switch with wireless capabilities. (Photo: Mr Resistor)

Conventional Dimmer Switches

Conventional dimmer switches are commonly found in most properties and consist of a round dimmer knob that can be turned clockwise or anti-clockwise to raise and lower the light levels respectively. The knob can also be pushed in to turn the lights on and off. There are many variations of this kind of dimmer, including push buttons, sliders and sensor pads, but they all effectively dim the lights up and down and turn them on and off.

Dimmer switches are generally mounted on switch plates in groups, or 'gangs'. While standard dimmer switch plates have as many as four dimmer switches, there are many larger versions available, up to and above twenty dimmers on a plate. However, it is important not to put too many dimmers on one plate since most people will not be able to remember which switch operates which circuit, and if there are too many dimmer switches on a plate, then more time needs to be spent setting the light levels within the room, and it is unlikely that most people will bother. In most cases it is best to keep the number of dimmers to a maximum of

A Lutron Lyneo slide dimmer switch. (Photo: Mr Resistor)

A push button switch, linked to a remote dimmer pack. (Photo: Mr Resistor)

four on one plate. If more are needed within a space, then it may be best to add a separate dimmer switch in another position to operate the remaining circuits. For example, in a kitchen/dining room it is worth splitting the switches for the two different areas. This reduces confusion and allows more localized control.

Conventional dimmer switches are excellent for most rooms. They give complete control of individual circuit brightness levels, and allow the precise tailoring of the lighting levels within a space at any time. They are simple and intuitive to use, and most people are familiar with them, so guests visiting the house and children will be able to use them as well. They cost less than more sophisticated dimmer systems, so there can be cost savings in using conventional dimmer switches. The main downfall is the limited number of circuits they can control, with too many dimmer switches proving confusing.

Rotary dimmer switches, the most conventional type, can be connected with standard on/off switches in two-way and intermediate circuits. The dimmer must always be in one of the two-way positions and never in the intermediate position. In some cases it is necessary to have dimmers and on/off switches on the same switch plate. Most manufacturers offer options for custom-made or modular systems to enable this. It is also possible to have modules made in the dimmer switch style, but they just switch on and off. The dimmer knob is pushed to turn the circuit on and off, but when it is rotated there is no dimming. Some manufacturers even make on/off dimmer modules to go in the intermediate position in multi-switch circuits.

Dimming of LEDs and Fluorescents

LED and fluorescent lamps generally cannot be dimmed using a standard dimmer and require specialist equipment and wiring to ensure that they are dimmable, and the light fittings must be fitted with a dimmable driver or ballast. If the product does not specifically state that it is dimmable, then it is most likely to be fitted with a switching only driver. There are five common methods of dimming these types of lights:

0–10V or 1–10V

These use a potentiometer to provide a reference voltage between 0V and 10V. The driver or ballast to which the lamp is connected will then vary the output of the lamp to match the voltage. If the potentiometer is set to 5V, then the light output would be 50 per cent. The mains voltage power supplied to the driver or ballast is controlled with a switch in addition to the potentiometer. The switch is used to turn the lights off, while the potentiometer is

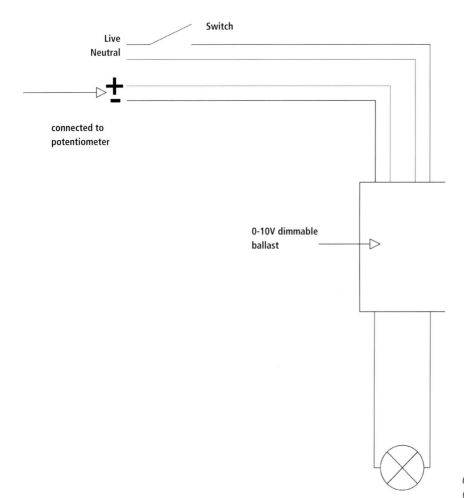

0–10V potentiometer wiring diagram. (Diagram: Marcus Steffen)

used to vary the light level. Some drivers and ballasts work using 0–10V, varying the brightness across the full range, so the lowest light output possible (which is not always 0 per cent) is achieved at 0V. Others use 1–10V, where the lowest brightness occurs at 1V, and anything below 1V will switch the lamp off. This will do away with the need for a separate switch, though it should be noted that power will be permanently supplied to the drivers in this case.

Digital Serial Interface (DSI)

DSI is a digital dimming system developed by Tridonic Atco as an alternative to 0–10V dimming. It sends a digital signal to the driver or ballast and, depending on the value of the digital signal, the driver or ballast will adjust its brightness accordingly. It has the ability to turn the lamp off by sending a zero signal, so a switch line is not required, though power will still be present at the light fittings at all times, so care should be taken during maintenance: even though the lamp is off, the ballast is not.

Digital Addressable Lighting Interface (DALI)

DALI was developed as an alternative open standard to DSI. As well as digital dimming, DALI allows addressable drivers and ballasts and monitoring of their current states. It is used extensively in commercial lighting. Each driver or ballast is given an address and can be individually controlled. This simplifies the wiring since the light fittings do not need to be split into predetermined circuits. The groupings can be chosen at the commissioning stage of the system. There is a maximum limit of sixty-four light fittings on a DALI wiring loop, sometimes called a DALI universe. As well as dimming and grouping control, DALI also allows monitoring of the lamp and driver/ballast state. This enables control systems to create reports of what lamps and drivers/ballasts are faulty and need replacing. This is extremely useful in very large commercial buildings where there are tenants and thousands of light fittings.

In residential properties DALI can seem like an economical option due to the cheap control system cost, but it is advisable to consider the full cost of the system, including commissioning. A professional programmer will be required to address all the light fittings and group them into different circuits. If these need to be changed, then the programmer will need to return and redo the grouping, normally at an additional cost. The other drawback of DALI in residential properties concerns the replacement of drivers/ballasts. The DALI system automatically addresses all light fittings. When a driver or ballast is changed, then all fittings on the DALI universe will normally need to be read-

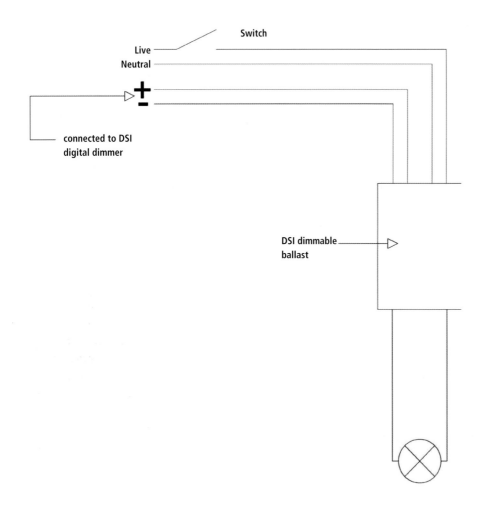

DSI wiring diagram. (Diagram: Marcus Steffen)

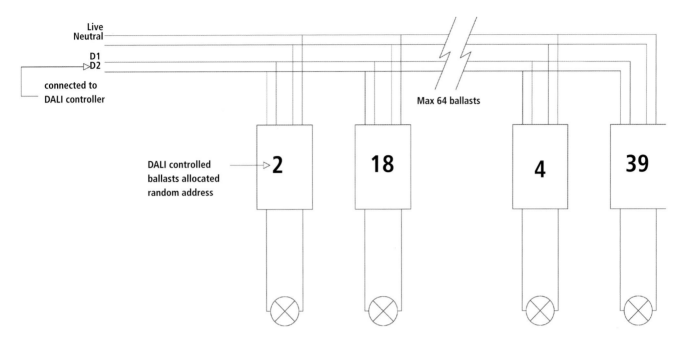

DALI wiring diagram, also showing random addressing. (Diagram: Marcus Steffen)

dressed. Again, this will require a programmer, and can result in very high after-care costs. Finally, it is not possible to dim incandescent or halogen lamps with DALI, since there is no driver or ballast for these lamp types.

Digital MultipleX (DMX)

DMX is another digital addressing system. This the most common method of controlling theatrical lighting, and it is regularly used for colour changing in residential and commercial properties. It requires a special controller to operate the lighting, which runs pre-set programs operating all drivers or ballasts linked to the system. A DMX system has 512 addresses in its universe, hence its full title DMX512. Each address can be dimmed up and down individually, allowing a large degree of flexibility. With colour-changing lighting three addresses are normally used, one for red, another for green and the final one for blue. On the individual drivers or ballasts it is possible to set the address on that unit using a binary code system. Each DIP switch on the unit will have a value, and the values of all the DIP switches set to 'on' are added up to create an address. If the unit is using more than one address, such as an RGB unit with three addresses,

then it uses an incremental numbering system: n, n+1, n+2, etc.

DMX wiring must be run in a ring, rather than split or radial wired. If the wiring has to be run in a radial fashion, then a DMX splitter must be used, which will ensure that all fittings on the different radials remain synchronized. A terminator must be fitted at the end of a DMX loop. This prevents clashing signals, which can cause a stutter effect in the lighting.

SwitchDIM

SwitchDIM is a simple method of dimming drivers or ballasts using a push button interface. A momentary switch is wired to the driver/ballast and when the contact is made the output will be changed. If it is a short contact, then the driver/ballast will switch off, but if the button is held down for a long contact the lighting will be dimmed up or down. All the drivers and ballasts require a permanent power supply to them, and a momentary switch rather than a conventional switch must be used. There is no way of knowing what light level the driver/ballast is set to, so it is not advisable to use a contact closure output from a control system to operate SwitchDIM drivers/ballasts.

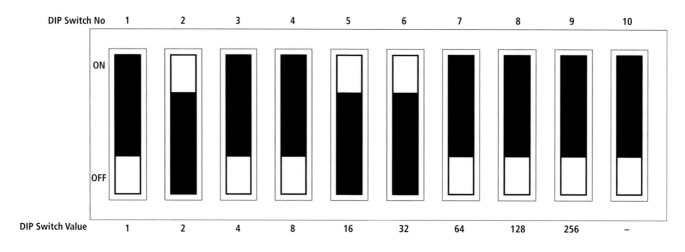

Example:
DIP switches 2, 5 and 6 are on.
Address No = 2+16+32 = 50

Diagram showing how binary code is generated from dip switches on a DMX driver. (Photo: Marcus Steffen)

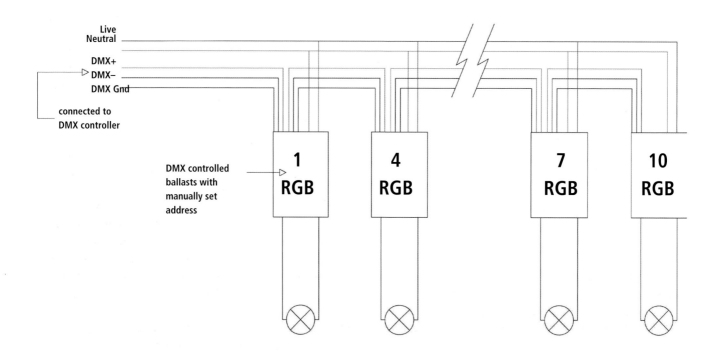

DMX wiring diagram. Note the terminator mounted at the end of the DMX link. (Diagram: Marcus Steffen)

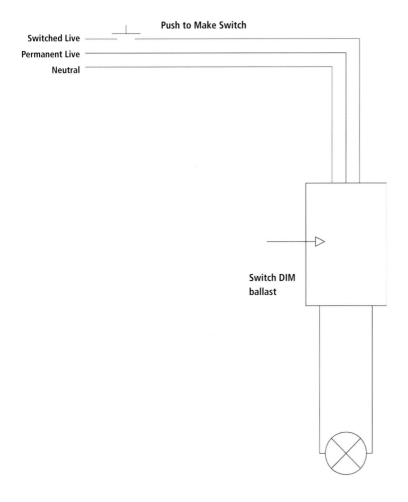

Push to Make Switch

Switched Live

Permanent Live

Neutral

Switch DIM
ballast

switches that are adjusted and saved for each scene, while others require a computer to program, sometimes with a professional programmer. When selecting a scene-setting system, it is important to find out what setting up is needed, and what control the user will have over these settings. If a professional programmer is required to attend the property every time changes are required, then this could prove very expensive. In some cases adjustment is possible from switches on the system, and a programmer is only required for the initial setting up. In many systems it is possible for the end user to program the system, but sometimes this can be a complex process. Discussing the whole process, from purchasing the system to having it commissioned, is very important, since once it is installed, it is difficult to return to conventional switching. Scene-setting systems do have many advantages over conventional switches and dimmers. Each scene can control many circuits, so rather than having a bank of eight dimmer switches on the wall, it is possible to have a small switch with three to five scenes, reducing the complexity of the switching on the wall. The scenes ensure that only the lighting that is needed is on at any time. This both increases the impact and effects of these light sources and saves energy since all unnecessary lights are switched off. Most scene-control systems have soft fades on and off, helping to create nice transitions to different moods and extending the life of the lamps. There will also be a scene to turn all the lighting off, so all the lights in the room can be switched off at the touch of one button.

It is very easy to get carried away with the number of scenes in a room. Generally, less is more. If there are ten scene buttons for a room, it will be very difficult to remember which one does what. Guests will be very confused as to how these switches work, as will less technically fluent members of a family. It is best to think of how the lighting will be used within a space and what will be required. For example, a kitchen requires a scene with bright lighting for cooking, a relaxed light for eating or general use, and a night-time setting for late night use, such as getting a glass of water. This would only be three scenes in all, plus an extra one to turn the

SCENE CONTROL

Scene control, sometimes known as scene-setting or mood control, is a very powerful tool for ensuring that the lighting is always at the right levels within a room. Scene-control systems do not have individual dimmers for lighting circuits on the walls, but rather have buttons that can operate a number of circuits at the same time. When a scene button is pressed, the controlled circuits adjust to pre-set levels, ensuring the lights are always at the right level for their use within the room. On a switch plate there will normally be multiple buttons offering different scenes for different purposes.

Scene control ensures that the lighting is always right for the interior decoration of a room and its intended purpose. Scene-control systems are inherently more complex than standard dimmer switches on the wall, so some setting up will be required and each scene needs to be programmed. With some control systems there is a central bank of dimmer

A bedroom
with good
general lighting
from recessed
downlights. (Photo:
Mr Resistor)

The same bedroom
with good ambient
and task lighting
from two bedside
table lamps. (Photo:
Mr Resistor)

Scenes and Circuit Level Settings

Scene	Circuit 1 Downlights	Circuit 2 Table Lamps	Circuit 3 Low-level night-lights
Bright	100 per cent	100 per cent	0 per cent
Relaxed	70 per cent	100 per cent	0 per cent
Intimate	20 per cent	60 per cent	0 per cent
Night	0 per cent	0 per cent	100 per cent

lighting off. It does not matter how many lighting circuits are in the room, they will all fit into these three scenes.

House Control Systems

House control systems extend the idea of scene control across the whole property. These systems generally require a programmer to commission them, but they allow much more control over how the lighting works. Normally anything can be done with the control of the lighting, but the key to having one of these systems is that they simplify the control of the lighting as much as possible. Many of the systems available can also incorporate blind and curtain control, and some even have audio-visual and thermostat controls.

House control systems have a centralized control processor. All the switches, buttons and dimmers are controlled from this processor. Dimmers are normally installed in large racks located in cupboards or utility rooms. There may be thirty to fifty dimmers per rack. Buttons are not linked to the dimmers directly, but rather send a signal to the processor. The processor then decides what happens when this button is pressed. This gives ultimate flexibility, since a button press can be set to do anything on the system. It may turn on a single circuit of lighting, but it might equally be a scene button, or even open a blind. This is all set up in the commissioning of the system. It is important to realize that there is this degree of flexibility to achieve the most out of the control system.

House control systems allow the switching of any lighting from anywhere in the house. Common controls available on these systems are an all-off switch by the front door, or a button that turns on holiday settings for the home. Scenes can be created not just for rooms but for whole areas. When a button is pressed by the front door, it may turn on the hall lights, but the kitchen and living room lights will also come on so that the home feels warm and inviting. These systems also have built-in time-clocks, meaning that lighting can be switched on and off at certain times. These time-clock functions can even be programmed from the actual use of the lighting on some systems, so that it replicates a real human presence when the house is empty. Alarm systems can also input signals into the lighting system, so that when the alarm goes off, whether relating to someone trespassing on the property or a fire, the lighting can be switched on, and the switches can be disabled so that an intruder cannot turn them off.

While whole house control has endless possibilities, it is worth noting that it is not suitable in all cases. It requires setting up by a professional programmer and in some cases this can be costly. If the end user of the home is not comfortable with lots of technology, the lighting controls may become overwhelming, and this can be very frustrating. If a house control system is to be used, it is crucial to have it programmed properly, otherwise it will not be worth spending the money on these systems.

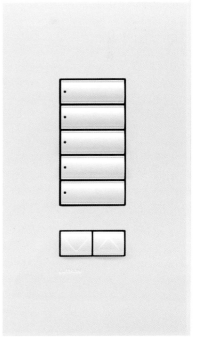

A Lutron architrave keypad used for scene setting (Diagram: Mr Resistor)

CHAPTER 11

CREATING A LIGHTING PLAN

Any lighting design should take into account the space and uses of the different rooms, and be tailored to them. The lighting in a room should highlight and complement it, and should bring out the best in the space. Without light, the room would not be visible, and with bland lighting it can feel uncomfortable and uninviting. With the combination of general, task, ambient and effect lighting in a space, texture and contrast can be introduced that bring out the features of the room and provide the right light to live in comfort.

When creating a home, it is important to make sure that the builders, architects, designers and clients all share the vision. This is one of the most difficult areas of the construction industry, and many projects have failed because of poor communication between the various parties involved. The basis of all communication when building a house is the architectural plans. These show how the house should be constructed, and provide the builder and subcontractors with all the information they need to carry out the construction. The architectural plans also form the basis of any contracts between the builder and the client. If something is incorrect on the plan, then this can result in extra costs and delays on a project. In the same vein, if the building work does not match the plans, then the contractors will be liable for these mistakes, and will need to correct them at their own cost. Almost every construction project runs into some problems as unforeseen issues arise, so even with a perfect set of plans it is important to maintain a good dialogue between all parties. Having a good set of clear plans

that contain all the necessary detail is very beneficial on any project, and will help all parties understand the work involved. As with any part of the construction process, the lighting needs to be shown on the architectural plans for the contractors to install correctly. If it is not shown, then the wiring will not be put in the right place, and it will be very costly to go back and correct it later on. There are three main docu-

OPPOSITE: Artwork lit with two adjustable downlights stands out from the darker surfaces around it.

RIGHT: A floor plan showing the lighting fittings, lighting circuits and switch. (Diagram: Marcus Steffen)

ments that need to be produced to ensure all the information is shown:

a lighting plan;
a load chart; and
a specification book.

These three documents provide the contractor with everything that is needed to carry out the installation of the lighting and ensure that it is working correctly. They form the basis of any lighting design. There may be extra information that can be provided, such as 3D concept sketches, but these are not necessary to carry out the building work.

LIGHTING PLAN

The lighting plan is the key ingredient for any lighting design. If there is one item of paperwork that is crucial, then this is it. A contractor should be able to get most of the work done with just a lighting plan, without needing the other details. It is only when using unconventional lighting or switches that the other two parts become important to getting the installation done correctly. All lighting plans contain the following details:

- positions of all the light fittings, shown with symbols on the drawing;
- lighting circuits, showing which light fittings are to be switched together;
- light switches; and
- a key detailing what each of the symbols on the plan means, and giving references to the specification book.

With all this information on the lighting plan, the electrician will be able to work out what cables need to be installed and where they need to be run to. The lighting plan should be as clear as possible and the lighting should stand out. It is best to show the lighting on a plan without any other services. If all the other services, such as electrics, plumbing and heating, etc., are shown on the plan with the lighting, then it can become 'lost' in the detail, and it is much more likely that something will be missed by the contractor. While it is the contractor's responsibility to ensure that all works shown on the plan are carried out, there is no reason to make it more complicated than necessary. A clear, well laid out plan helps

to ensure that the work is carried out correctly the first time round, making everyone happy.

Light fittings should be shown on the plans with different symbols, and it is important to have a symbol for each type of fitting. For example, if there are fixed, adjustable and waterproof downlights in a lighting plan, then they should be marked with three different symbols. They may all use a circle to signify that they are downlights, but either colour coding or letter/number notations need to be added to differentiate between the different types.

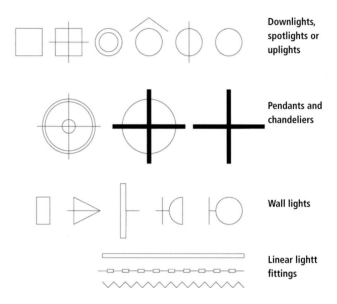

Downlights, spotlights or uplights

Pendants and chandeliers

Wall lights

Linear lightt fittings

Various symbols used to show light fittings on architectural plans. (Diagram: Marcus Steffen)

The light fittings should be placed in the correct locations, and dimensions should also be shown for placement. It is not normally possible to produce dimensions that are 100 per cent accurate at the planning stage, but there are a number of ways to show how lighting should be positioned without showing the exact spacing between fittings. For example, if three pendants are to be placed in a row, with the centre one in the middle of the room, then it could be noted on the plan that the centre one is to be centred in the middle of the room, and the other two placed 500mm to either side. This relative dimensioning allows for flexibility in the building dimensions while ensuring the lights are placed in the correct locations. When laying out the lighting on the plan, it is easy to start lining up all the fittings in neat symmetrical patterns. This does work in open, generic spaces, especially in offices where general light needs to be spread across the entire space, but in the home it is very rare that the entire building is symmetrical all the way down to the furniture. When choosing the positions of lights, they should be tailored to where the light is going to fall in the space, not to where the light fitting will be. People rarely notice that light fittings do not line up, but they will certainly notice if the light patterns are wrong, or if there is inadequate light over a work surface.

Sometimes it is not possible to show all the information on the architectural plans, and fittings must be shown on elevation drawings and on detail drawings of installations. The heights of wall lights need to be specified to ensure they are placed correctly. They can be marked on the plan (for example, with a note reading, 'wall light to be mounted 1700mm from finished floor level), but in some cases, especially where there are different wall lights and switches next to each other, it may be necessary to show them on an elevation drawing. Elevations can also be very helpful for showing how lighting will be built into furniture and shelving, since this will not be clear from the plan view. Detail drawings can show how to construct certain features and their size requirements. This is important when lighting is being built into furniture, so that the carpenters can ensure it is constructed correctly. It may also be required for ceiling trough details on anything that requires construction work beyond either cutting a hole or fixing directly onto a surface.

An elevation showing the position of the bed and how the wall lights and switches could be laid out around it. (Photo: Marcus Steffen)

Lighting Circuits

Lighting circuits are the groupings of light fittings onto a switch, and on the plans they show which lights will be switched or dimmed together. Knowing which light fittings can be wired together and how many will be on a circuit is vital for the electrician. Circuits are normally shown on a lighting plan by a line marked out between the light fittings. It can be a solid or dotted line, and may be curved or straight. It is normally better to use curved lines, since they will then not be confused with walls or other structures shown on the plan. As well as the line connecting all the fittings on a lighting circuit, there should also be a unique circuit number. This is very important, since it identifies the lighting circuit in other documentation, such as a quote for goods or on the load chart. Without individual circuit numbers, there can be some confusion over what is being referred to, and this can lead to mix-ups in the installation. For example, if there are three circuits with downlights in a kitchen, they need some form of notation to differentiate them. When laying out the lighting circuit lines, it is advantageous to show them as clearly as possible, and avoid having the circuit lines crossing over each other unnecessarily since this can make the plan very confusing. With a little forethought, it is normally possible to draw all the circuit lines without them crossing over.

Lighting circuits are shown with a line connecting the light fittings together and a circuit label. (Diagram: Marcus Steffen)

In some cases a circuit is not shown with a line connecting the fittings but rather with a notation next to each light fitting on the drawing. All light fittings in a room may have a code of C1, C2, etc., and this number indicates to which circuit they are connected. This can save on the drawing, and may be helpful in a room with multiple circuits, but there are some problems with this method. The first is that it is not clear at the initial viewing of the plan which light fittings are operated together. Each light fitting has to be looked at individually and the circuits worked out. This can take extra time, and also make the plans more difficult to explain to other people involved in the project. Another problem is that it becomes very easy to miss a fitting on a plan. Especially in complex lighting plans, there may be light fittings on the same circuit scattered all over a room, and if one is missed and not wired, then this can cause issues later on. It is the contractor's responsibility to ensure the fittings are wired as on the plan, but it is best to give them as clear a plan as possible before starting the work.

Controls

The switches also need to be shown on a lighting plan. It is important to make it clear which switch operates which light-

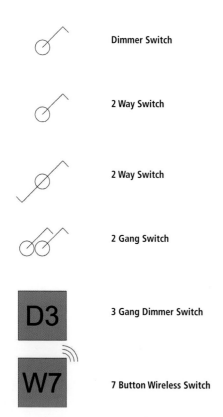

Dimmer Switch

2 Way Switch

2 Way Switch

2 Gang Switch

D3   3 Gang Dimmer Switch

W7   7 Button Wireless Switch

Examples of commonly used switch symbols.
(Diagram: Marcus Steffen)

ing circuit, and also what type of switch is being used. In a two-way and intermediate circuit it is best to specify that one of the switches will be an intermediate. The most common way of showing switches is by having a symbol for each individual switch or dimmer, grouped together in areas. The total number is the size of the switch that will need to be ordered. To show the link between switches and lighting circuits, the drawn circuit line is normally shown contacting each switch that will operate it. This is fine in rooms with one switch position and a few circuits, but can become very confusing in open plan spaces or rooms with multiple switching positions. In this case it is best to show the switches on the walls, and have a circuit number written next to each switch. This helps prevent the plan becoming confusing with too many circuit lines drawn on it.

The switch notation should also contain details of its type and any special requirements. Switches and phase dimmers work using standard wiring, but if a 0–10V dimmer or another special type is being used then this must be noted. Every dimmer should be identified, and there should be an additional note on the plan detailing how the wiring differs from the conventional. It should also be noted if a special back box is required for any switches, since these need to be ordered early on in the project and installed before the walls are plastered and painted.

If a non-conventional control system is being used, then the actual keypads on the walls may not have any physical link to the circuits they are operating. In this case, it would be incorrect to show circuit cables linking the switch positions and the lighting circuits. Instead, the centralized switching/dimming panels should be indicated, and should show which circuits are being controlled from there. It is not normally practical to show every circuit line going back to a centralized location, and it is best to have a separate list of circuits on the plan. If the wall switches are to be wired, then this should be shown. Most control systems use some sort of data cable to link to all the switches, and this should also be shown on the plan. Likewise, if the switches are wireless, then this should be indicated to show that no cable is required.

Key

The final, and essential, part of the lighting plan is the key. This shows what each symbol on the plan means, and provides a reference point between the plan and the specification book. If a symbol is not detailed on the key, then the contractor may

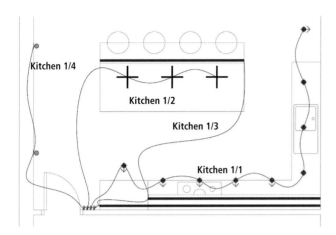

The circuit lines are brought back to the switches that operate them to show the link. (Diagram: Marcus Steffen)

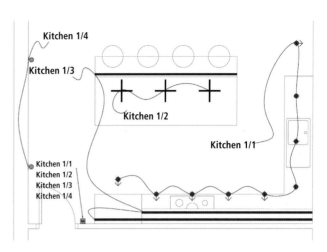

The switches are labelled to indicate which circuits they are operating. (Diagram: Marcus Steffen)

not know what it means, and may not know what to install in that position. The key should consist of at least a copy of each symbol and a part code that it refers to. This could be a general reference to a light fitting (such as 'wall light') or it could be a specific part code for a light fitting or switch. It is also useful to include details of what is being shown. For example, 'DOWNLIGHT A – LED adjustable recessed downlight, 10W, 2700K warm white, requires 350mA driver'. This gives enough detail as to what is required without the need to refer to the specification book. Normally it is not possible to put this level of detail on a plan until the light fittings have been finalized, and this is why the specification book is very important. If a particular light fitting is specified, then it is possible to add any special notes to the key pertaining to its installation. This may be a special back box, or an indication that the fitting must be installed before the wall is plastered. This saves having to write individual notes on the plan every time the fitting is used.

A key showing both a symbol, a part code and a description of each light fitting and switch. (Diagram: Marcus Steffen)

KEY

 FRTRD50WHTGU101P – Waterproof downlight

FRTRD50 WHT – Round trimless downlight

 FRTSQ50 WHT – Square trimless downlight

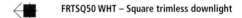 FTT300 WHT – Triple trimless downlight

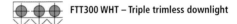 LEDHLF236-1 WARM –Large downlight

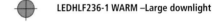 BARI 0340 – Waterproof Wall Light

CUBA 0273 – Wall Light

FUJI – Bathroom Mirror Light

TR8144 THL – Wall Light

MOSTO 0813 – Wall Light

AL4020 W.WH –Low Level Wall Light

R* Rocker Switch – *= number of switches

D* Dimmer Switch – *= number of dimmers

LOAD CHART

The load chart acts as a breakdown of all the light circuits in the property. It takes the form of a spreadsheet and gives details on the lighting circuit numbers, their locations and the light fittings used, as well as the loadings and dimming types. This helps define how each circuit will be operated, and also gives the electrician details on the total power required, allowing the consumer units (sometimes referred to as fuse boxes) and other electrical protection components required within the home to be designed. It also provides a document where notes can be made on the different circuits for the installer's guidance. There is a key list of information that is required for each lighting circuit:

- room;
- circuit number;
- description;
- light fittings used and their quantities;
- load per fitting (in Watts);
- load per circuit (in Watts);
- lighting type (incandescent, LED, fluorescent, etc.); and
- dimming type (phase/standard, 0–10V, DALI, etc.).

This information is important for the electrician to ensure the correct cabling is installed in the property and the consumer unit and other electrical equipment is of the correct specification. The load chart can act as a helpful reference to identify which light fittings are used in different rooms, and is useful for calculating the number of light fittings of each type that need to be ordered. The load chart is also an essential reference tool if a sophisticated control system is being installed. It allows the specifier to ensure that all the right equipment is used for the light and dimming types, and that the capacity is high enough for the loads on the lighting.

SPECIFICATION BOOK

A specification book is a catalogue of all the fixtures and fittings that are to be installed in a building. This not only covers lighting but also plumbing, doors, windows and a whole host of other details. It acts as a reference guide for the contractor to ensure that the correct fittings are installed in the right areas, with information about purchasing the fittings from manufacturers. The specification book consists of at least one specification sheet for each fitting. Sometimes there are more if there are accessories for a fitting or special installation instructions. A specification for light fittings almost always contains the following information:

- a reference from the lighting plan;
- a picture;
- a description;
- the manufacturer;
- its part code;
- dimensions, including any extra details, such as burial tubes;
- adjustable details, such as rotation and tilt angles;
- light emission data (lumen/peak candela output, or a lamp reference if this is separate);
- electrical specifications (voltage, maximum wattage, lamp type, life);
- IP rating; and
- class rating (I, II or III).

There may also be additional information, such as schematic and wiring diagrams, installation guides and extra technical details. The information required will depend on the type of light fitting specified. Most manufacturers have ready-made specification sheets for their light fittings, and these can just be inserted into the project specification book. In some cases the specification sheet will need to be manually assembled, especially where custom-made fittings are being included.

INDEX

0-10V and 1-10V   145
2 amp sockets   41
5 amp sockets   41

ambient lighting   57–61
  bathroom   94–96
  kitchen   77–80
  living room   113–114
Amps   10
anti glare baffle   32
artwork   35, 61–65

baffle   32
barn doors   34
bathroom   85–101
bathroom zones   86–87
bedroom   127–137
bookcase   107–111

candela   9
chandelier   27–28, 117–121
children's bedrooms   136
cold cathode   24
colour   10, 50–52
colour change   17, 67, 75
colour rendering index   11
controls   139–151, 156
  bathroom   100–101
  bedroom   136–137
  dining room   125
  kitchen   82–83
  living room   115
correlated colour temperature   10, 50–52
cupboard internal lighting   131–133
current   10

daylight   10, 50

desk lighting   111–112
digital addressable lighting interface (DALI)   146–147
digital multiplex (DMX)   147–148
digital serial interface (DSI)   146
dimmers   143–147
dining room   117–125
direct light   47–49

effect lighting   61
  bathroom   97–100
  kitchen   77–80
efficacy   9
electric potential   10
extractor fan   101
eyeball   32

fibre optics   24, 66
floor lights   40–41, 123
fluorescent   19–23, 75
framing projector   35, 63

gang   144
general lighting   52–54
  bathroom 86–90
  bedroom   133–136
  dining   123–124
  kitchen   77
  living room 103–107
gimbal   32
glare   32, 47
glass   58
gobo projector   35

halogen   14–16
holiday control   151
humidity sensor   101
illuminance   9, 53

incandescent 13-14
indirect light 47-49
ingress protection (IP) rating 86
intermediate 140–141
interna 10, 50

Kelvin 10
key 156–157
kitchen 69–83

lamps 13–25
LED 16–19
LED driver 18
LED strips 44–45, 75, 109–111, 133
light emitting diodes 16–19
lighting circuit 155
lighting plan 153–157
linear lighting 44
living room 103–115
load 9
load chart 158
low level wall lights 38–39, 96
low voltage track 35
lumen 9
luminous flux 9
luminous Intensity 9
Lux 9, 53

metal halide 25
mirrors 90-93
mounting height 38

night light 96

open plan spaces 113

passive infra-red sensors 101, 143
pendants 27–28, 69, 117–121
picture lighting 35
picture lights 63
PIR sensor 101, 143
power 9

receiver 141
recessed downlight 28–32, 121–122, 133–134
    ceiling construction 30–31
    fire rated ceilings 31
    positioning 53

recessed uplight 41–44, 65, 95
RGB 17, 67

safety regulations 86
scene control 149–151
scoop 32
SELV 86
Shadow 47
shelves 107–111
sofas 103-106
specification book 158
spotlights 32–34
star ceilings 24, 66
suspended wire systems 34–37
SwitchDIM 147
switches 140–143
symbols 154

table 117–123
table lights 40–41, 130
task lighting 54–57
    bathroom mirrors 90–93
    bedroom 127–131
    desk 111–112
    kitchen 69–76
texture 59, 96–97
timers 143, 151
track 34–36, 122–123
    single circuit 35
    three circuit 35
transmitter 141
tungsten halogen 14–16
two-way 140–141

under cupboard lighting 56, 72–76

vaulted ceilings 81

voltage 10, 86
Volts 10

wall lights 37–39, 123, 134–136
wardrobe 131–133
waterproof 86
Watt 9
wire systems 34–37, 123
wireless switches 141–142